MW01061701

What is
Architectural History?

What is History? series

What is Architectural History?

ANDREW LEACH

polity

Copyright © Andrew Leach 2010

The right of Andrew Leach to be identified as Author of this Work has been asserted in accordance with the UK Copyright, Designs and Patents Act 1988.

First published in 2010 by Polity Press

Polity Press
65 Bridge Street
Cambridge CB2 1UR, UK

Polity Press
350 Main Street
Malden, MA 02148, USA

All rights reserved. Except for the quotation of short passages for the purpose of criticism and review, no part of this publication may be reproduced, stored in a retrieval system, or transmitted, in any form or by any means, electronic, mechanical, photocopying, recording or otherwise, without the prior permission of the publisher.

ISBN-13: 978-0-7456-4456-1
ISBN-13: 978-0-7456-4457-8(pb)

A catalogue record for this book is available from the British Library.

Typeset in 10.5 on 12 pt Sabon
by Toppan Best-set Premedia Limited
Printed and bound in Great Britain by MPG Books Group Limited, Bodmin, Cornwall

The publisher has used its best endeavours to ensure that the URLs for external websites referred to in this book are correct and active at the time of going to press. However, the publisher has no responsibility for the websites and can make no guarantee that a site will remain live or that the content is or will remain appropriate.

Every effort has been made to trace all copyright holders, but if any have been inadvertently overlooked the publisher will be pleased to include any necessary credits in any subsequent reprint or edition.

For further information on Polity, visit our website:
www.politybooks.com

Contents

List of illustrations

Acknowledgements

I wish to thank Andrea Drugan of Polity for the encouragement and forbearance that saw this book get off the ground – and land again. I first prepared its content for a series of seminar papers at the University of Queensland, Australia, and I am grateful to my colleagues in the School of Architecture for their advice and encouragement, and the students of my 2008 and 2009 M.Arch classes for their provocations and intense discussions. A research grant from the School of Architecture furthermore enabled me to cover the cost of illustrations. I hope the many individuals who have offered me valuable suggestions, corrections and criticism will forgive the necessary economy of naming three readers who had a decisive impact on the book's final form, specifically John Harwood, Pieter Martens and Paul Walker. Polity's anonymous proposal and manuscript reviewers were right on the mark in their criticisms, and the book benefited substantially from their contribution. The University of Queenland's Centre for the History of European Discourses provided stimulating company and a quiet place to work when I needed it – thanks especially to Peter Cryle, Ian Hunter and Ryan Walter. John Macarthur helped me to iron out several of my positions; the book records my side of our occasional but stimulating discussions on its theme. I owe a deep debt to Bart Verschaffel and my former colleagues at Ghent University, where I was fortunate to return as a visiting research fellow as I put the final edits to bed. All of these debts notwithstanding, unless I indicate otherwise the views in this book are my own, as are the errors of fact and omission. Ben Wilson helped with editing of the first draft, and the production team at Polity expertly saw this book into press. Thanks go particularly to Jonathan Skerrett, Lauren Mulholland and Leigh Mueller. My family – Ruth, Katie, Chelsea and Amelia – have offered the right blend of encouragement and distraction. Ruth, especially, has once more given me her unflinching support, for which I remain infinitely grateful. Our daughter Amelia was not yet born when I committed to this title. For better or worse it has been in the background of her first two years, and it seems only right that I dedicate it to her.

How to use this book

This book is written as an introduction to the conceptual questions faced by those who write architectural history and study the work of architectural historians. As such, it assumes some basic knowledge of architectural history, its chronologies, canon and geographies, such as the reader might find in a more general survey of the history of architecture. Readers of this book might be taking courses or conducting research in architectural history while attached to a school of architecture, or in a department of art history; or they might be undertaking a history programme where buildings and city plans are thought to evidence historical phenomena that do not originate in architecture. *What is Architectural History?* introduces some of the key issues that have shaped the way in which historical knowledge of architecture has been formed, rallied and disseminated over the last century or so, and aims to direct inquisitive readers to other writing that explores aspects of this subject and its major figures in greater depth.

Introduction

In the preface to *Renaissance und Barock* (1888), one of the founding modern histories of architecture, the young Swiss art historian Heinrich Wölfflin explained the intentions of his book:

> The subject of this study is the disintegration of the Renaissance. It is intended to be a contribution to the history of style rather than of individual artists. My aim was to investigate the symptoms of decay and perhaps to discover in the 'capriciousness and the return to chaos' a law which would vouchsafe one an insight into the intimate workings of art. This, I confess, is to me the real aim of art history.[1]

We might not now agree with Wölfflin's views that the works of architecture appearing in Rome during the sixteenth and seventeenth centuries describe a descent from the High Renaissance into a state of chaos. Nor would we find it remarkable to write the histories of art and architecture as other than the history of painters, sculptors and architects. Wölfflin's brief words of introduction nevertheless raise a number of questions. How, for example, and why should historians study architecture? How does architecture change over time as a concept, art and institution? And why does change occur? Because of factors internal to architecture itself, or because of the forces to which architects are subject?

In setting out the terms for the academic study of architectural history, Wölfflin inscribed a series of concepts and questions that have proved fundamental to the architectural historian's practice. Even as architectural historians have left Wölfflin and his methodology behind, developed new approaches and cultivated fresh territories of enquiry, they remain indebted to this initial systematization and intellectualization of architecture as a modern historical field. Nonetheless, as a discipline architectural history echoes a common problem faced by many historical disciplines and specializations: there is as little agreement on what architectural history is and how it should be done as on what architecture is and how it should be made.

1   Il Gesù, Rome, officially the Chiesa del Santissimo Nome di Gesù all'Argentina. Construction commenced 1568; consecrated 1584. Principal architects Giacomo Barozzi da Vignola and Giacomo della Porta.

This book is concerned with the form of architectural historiography that emerged in the mode of a discipline at the start of the twentieth century and persists in today's universities and learned societies. I use the term 'discipline' lightly; there is by no means a consensus on whether architectural history is a discipline in any autonomous sense, even if one might talk hesitantly of its 'disciplinarity'. Few of those describing themselves as architectural historians were trained first in the history of architecture as such, rather specializing after initial undergraduate formations in architecture, art history or some other related field. This does not undermine the persistence of a coherent line of enquiry or the presence of an equally coherent body of work concerned with the history of architecture served by these specialists, range as they might from consultants in the restoration and preservation of architectural heritage through to academics concerned with architecture's intellectual history. It does, however, raise a number of issues that this book will explore.

Architecture is a popular subject that receives a great deal of non-specialist attention. In setting some restrictions on our discussion we would be wise not to underplay the large audience for architectural history of all kinds. We could narrowly define the academic practice of architectural history as the teaching and research activity concerned with the history of architecture that we find in universities, academies, museums and research institutes: doctoral students preparing theses and scholars writing books and articles.[2] It would be foolish, though, to overlook the material gathered and processed by the vast number of enthusiasts, hobbyists and dilettantes who share the academic's interest in architectural history.

Many of these non-academics are architects who enjoy a privileged perspective from which to delve into the deep past of their own profession. Professional authors like journalists, biographers and travel writers likewise regularly take architecture as their subject. Their contribution to architectural historiography appears in coffee-table books, architect-biographies and guidebooks – it is often derivative of existing scholarship, but not universally so. Local historians, too, write on architecture when their subjects relate strongly to the built environment. For example, a religious community might identify with a church building or convent, a university community with a college complex or campus. Archaeologists and historians of other specializations will regularly write on architecture when built works, interiors, architectural documents or city plans shed light on issues that are pertinent to their own respective disciplines and specializations.

This is not to mention the research undertaken around the practical tasks of restoring and preserving historic monuments and places, which often functions as the backbone of local architectural history. We recall, too, the comprehensive guidebooks to a region's architecture, like Guilio Lorenzetti's 1926 guide to Venice and its environs, or the Buildings of England series initiated by Nikolaus Pevsner in 1951, or the Buildings of the United States, the volumes of which have been appearing under the direction of the Society of Architectural Historians since 1993.[3]

All of these writers might share the architectural historian's interest in architecture, but will not necessarily participate in the intellectual traditions, access the methods or advance the questions that have proven central to architectural history as a modern academic field. The studies encompassed by the categories introduced above have nonetheless widened the audience for architecture and its history by piquing interest with notable details and connecting the particular and the peculiar with the general and the significant. However academic architectural historians might account for such studies as these, they demonstrate a form of historiography that exceeds the strict borders of scholarly activity as it can be found in the university, the programmes of museums and research institutes, and in the specialized forums[4] and scholarly journals[5] that lend architectural history its institutional form.

In this book I wish to cast architectural history as a field of study that draws on the widespread general interest and investment in architecture, monuments and cities while being subject, at a professional and academic level, to disciplinary rigours. This form of architectural historiography constitutes an enquiry into the past of architecture that pays varying degrees of attention to its usefulness for those who make architecture. Within this general constraint, my scope is intended to be catholic, using a range of approaches and

examples through which to consider the intellectual limits
and problems that affect the work of architectural historians.
Insofar as the question *What is Architectural History?* must
be asked of something, I direct it to the modern, academic
field of study instigated in the mode of cultural history and
art history that gained widespread currency from the end of
the nineteenth century.

That the very concept of architecture has more recently
expanded to become available as an analogy for corporate
structure, knowledge, communications and law is not, historically speaking, a new test for the field. The most enduring
and curious challenges faced by architectural historians have
concerned writing into history a field that is marked by conceptual and technical fluidity. There is little in architecture
that is consistent across all time and geography: appearance,
building technology, materials, uses, status and so on. Where
some have found it important to see fundamental differences
and ruptures between the Industrial Revolution and that
which followed, others have been content to posit longer
continuities that begin in the Renaissance or even the medieval world and implicate the work of present-day architects.
Others still have taken an even longer view that the activity
of building, irrespective of the values, intentions or status
projected by or ascribed to the buildings themselves, is the
material of a history of architecture as the history of building,
space-making or inhabitation. Matters of historical perspective are considered below. These frameworks have occasionally resulted in anachronism, and at other times have exposed
anachronisms in the work of others. In either case, as we
shall see, architectural history has regularly taken on the
form of a mirror – a mirror portraying a field of architecture
into which architecture itself peers in order to define itself
historically, a mirror held insistently before it by the
historian.

Surprisingly few books attempt a geographically inclusive
view of the methods and limits of architectural historiography, but the local development of many countries and regions
has come under close scrutiny. David Watkin's *The Rise of
Architectural History* (1980) and Simona Talenti's *L'histoire
de l'architecture en France* (2000) are both excellent surveys

concerned with important disciplinary geographies: France, Great Britain, Germany, Austria and Switzerland.[6] The anthology 'Problemi generali e problemi di metodologia storico-critico' was developed by Bruno Zevi and Paolo Portoghesi as a teaching tool; it offers a vital survey of texts concerned with method and other historiographical problems.[7] Likewise the special issue of *Architectural Design*, 'On the Methodology of Architectural History' (1981), is now a classic survey of approaches and voices.[8] A number of special issues of the *Journal of the Society of Architectural Historians* (*JSAH*) edited by Eve Blau[9] and Zeynep Çelik[10] from the end of the 1990s conduct a broad international survey of teaching, research and institutions in the field of architectural history. The American community of architectural historians has been especially mindful of its intellectual and institutional heritage, particularly in the period following the celebration in 1990 of fifty years of the SAH.[11] Great Britain, France, Germany, the Netherlands, Italy, Australia and New Zealand[12] have likewise evidenced concern with the conceptual and institutional bases of national or regional structures for supporting the work of architectural historians.

The tendency of recent years to explore the intellectual biographies of historians of architecture has yielded many significant insights into the means by which the work of these individuals contributed to the field. Reyner Banham, Sir John Summerson, Henry Russell Hitchcock, Pevsner, Zevi, Colin Rowe, Manfredo Tafuri and others have been subject to posthumous analysis regarding the relevance of their work to the practice of contemporary architects, theoreticians and historians of architecture. Panayotis Tounikiotis's *The Historiography of Modern Architecture* (1999) is a key study on the historiography of architectural modernism. So too is Anthony Vidler's *Histories of the Immediate Present* (2008), which probes deeply and perceptively into the work of four influential and mainly post-war historians who remained engaged with the polemics of contemporary architecture: Emil Kaufmann, Rowe, Banham and Tafuri.[13] We will encounter in the following pages a number of these later figures and the critical and scholarly attention they attract.

In a slightly different genre, Harry Francis Mallgrave's *Modern Architectural Theory* (2005) is one of the most important thematic studies in architecture's intellectual history of the last twenty years, adding considerable insight to the field surveyed authoritatively by Hanno-Walter Kruft in his *Geschichte der Architekturtheorie* (1985).[14] Tafuri's 1968 study *Teorie e storia dell'architettura* conducts a broad appraisal of the changing status of history within architectural culture since the fifteenth century, simultaneously offering a theoretical reflection on the historian's tools and tasks within that same culture.[15] It remains unrivalled as a theoretical reflection on the architectural historian's work.

As a library, these books and others that share their sense of disciplinary enquiry have made a number of distinct but interrelated incursions into the questions of what architectural history is and has been, how architectural historians as individuals or schools have conducted their practice, what constitutes historical knowledge for architecture, and what of architecture's intellectual or theoretical activity ought to be understood as historical. As such, they form an imposing context for this book, which seeks in turn to show how elements and sections of that library address those finer points to which I can at best allude.

What is Architectural History? comprises five chapters. The first considers a number of the rhetorical, analytical and historicist traditions from which modern architectural history has taken clues for its own limits and concerns. Whatever allegiance these approaches hold to modern and contemporary disciplines, this chapter demonstrates that many of the conflicts and complexities encountered by architectural historians in the twentieth and twenty-first centuries owe something to the diverse origins from which architectural history first drew as it entered the university as a structured field of study. The next chapter then considers several of the strategies by which historians narrate the past and systematize it according to critical categories, such as stylistic unity and change, period or the architectural œuvre. Leading on from these observations, the third chapter turns to the theme of evidence, its implications for the conceptualization of architectural history, and the tools and tasks this suggests for the architectural historian. The fourth chapter steps into the question of instrumentality or operativity by considering the relationship of architectural history to its professional audience, and the conceptual problems raised by anachronisms, historical traditions and the infiltration of architecture's 'project' into the domain of architectural history. This tendency among modernist historians of architecture drew much criticism later in the twentieth century, but we will consider it as an issue particular to an architectural culture that sometimes struggles to draw a clear line between production, reflection and critique. This moves us towards the final chapter, which studies the recent history of architectural historiography and the impact of architecture's 'theory moment' on its historians.[16]

Naturally, this leads us to reflect on the present day and the difficult question, 'what is architectural history, now?' On this point, the American architectural theorist K. Michael Hays recently wrote,

> The role of the historian is not principally to describe buildings or architects, to produce biographies, explications, and specialised commentaries – though we do that, too. The role of the historian is rather to be concerned with the larger conditions on which architectural knowledge and action is made possible: with the multiple agencies of culture in their ideological and historical and worldly forms.[17]

To understand how architectural history can be conceptually unified across the period bracketed at one end by this view and at the other by Wölfflin's words quoted at the outset is not, at first glance, such a difficult task considering the grounding effect of building as architectural historiography's basic material. But, as we will see, the ready availability of architectural history's tools and materials beyond any discernible core that the historian might assign to architecture is matched by the architectural historian's own bower-bird tendencies to draw from surrounding disciplines and to learn, above all, from his or her subject: the work of architecture and the intellectual, artistic, and technical cultures in which it has existed historically and continues to exist in the present, and the practically unlimited claims made by architecture on culture per se.

1
Foundations of a modern discipline

Antiquarians, historians, architects and archaeologists have long studied the architecture of the past. To look at architecture has meant looking at buildings and cities, artefacts and ruins, historical monuments and monumental sculptures, and to wonder how they came to be what they are. Architecture also offers a lasting mirror image of the people who commissioned, made and lived in and around it. When we already know something of them from other sources, understanding how and why they built enriches our knowledge of them. For as long as the architecture of the past has interested people in the present, the questions posed of it by scholars and students of all calibres have ranged wide. And so when architectural history emerged in German-speaking universities more than a century ago as part of the new discipline of art history, it borrowed tools, conceptual frameworks and imperatives from a range of places, but especially from archaeology, philology and architecture itself. Many of these tools, frameworks and imperatives have been adapted by successive generations of architectural historians to the extent that we can speak of them as now belonging properly to architectural history.

If architectural history is, in one sense, a democratic subject, available to anyone, it has nevertheless enjoyed privileged attention from its parent disciplines, which in turn have together shaped the modern academic discipline. Since the eighteenth century, for instance, architectural history has been taught to aspiring architects in schools and academies of architecture, grounding students in the past of their future profession, constructing and defending a canon of great works, and formulating and defining traditions – and the classical tradition above all. Art historians have long treated architecture as one of the visual arts, so that architects sat alongside painters, sculptors and printmakers – all artists. As the literary genre of the artist biography gave way to a 'scientific' art history, this convention remained firmly in place from the end of the nineteenth century as works of architecture became subject to formal and iconographic readings. Since the eighteenth century, archaeologists have scoured ancient building sites around the Mediterranean, Aegean, Adriatic and Red Seas. The architecture of the medieval era, too, has presented archaeologists with rich problems. In the British Isles and across northern and central Europe, study of the middle ages nourished early courses in the history of art and architecture and informed the first practices of architectural restoration and preservation. In Germany and Britain alike it underpinned a turn to Romanticism and nationalism. The nascent germanophone academic field of cultural history from the mid nineteenth century regarded architecture as evidence of culture, a resource equivalent to the history and 'science' of the visual and plastic arts. In this setting, architecture, as readily as printmaking, could help historians to understand the workings of culture and civilization. Buildings were documents that were best understood alongside other kinds of documents.

In their translation, many of these historiographical and analytical traditions now serve distinct ends for historians of architecture. Over the last century and a half, architectural history has emerged as a field of study in its own right. Some regard it as a discipline, with its own knowledge, questions and tools. Others understand the history of architecture as an inherently interdisciplinary venture. Others still treat architectural history as a specialization within the larger disciplines of architecture, art history, archaeology and history. Even those figures who have argued stringently for the disciplinary autonomy of architectural history find it difficult to isolate an incontestable core that remains unmuddied by multiform beginnings.

Defining architecture historically

Some scholars of architectural history defer to a canon of significant architects and buildings. Many would now rail against such a position, especially after the 1980s and 1990s and the upheavals of post-structuralist relativization that these decades witnessed across the humanities – and in the architectural humanities no less. The canon nonetheless has its uses, even if they are ultimately rhetorical.[1] Writers still quote the aphorism with which Pevsner famously began *An Outline of European Architecture* (1943): 'A bicycle shed is a building; Lincoln Cathedral is a piece of architecture.'[2] Whether or not one trusts these categories and what Pevsner does with them, they (and he) offer a familiar distinction between what architecture is and what it is not. This then acts as a starting point for separating out the finer conceptual and categorical distinctions that shape what falls in and beyond the remit of architectural history. Much of the twentieth-century history of architectural historiography is informed by this basic distinction, its application to historical problems, the historical judgements on which it rests, and the disagreements that gather around it.

There is great disagreement, too, over the set of buildings deemed fundamental to an architect's historical education, an art historian's knowledge of architecture, an anthropologist's study of traditional communities, a military historian's knowledge of castellated fortresses, an economic historian's appreciation of how building, urban planning and trade interact, or a church historian's understanding of architecture's expression of the liturgy or reaction to the dictates of the Curia – to name just a few examples. No one position has an inherently stronger claim than any other, even if the architect can claim privileged insight into historical works. Architecture is sometimes studied in its own terms, but is just as often tabled as evidence for problems that are not architectural in nature. A survey of houses built in the 1920s can tell us much about social and domestic arrangements, the structuring of class and gender roles, and geographical differences on these issues. They can tell us about technology and its repercussions for domestic life, patterns of consumption and standards of taste. Where architecture might hold

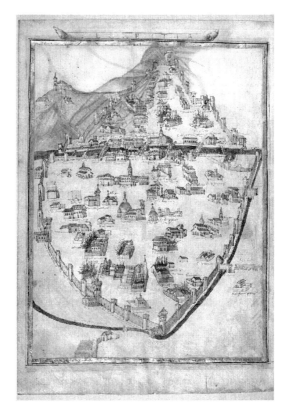

2   *Florentia*, rendering intended to illustrate Ptolemy's *Geografia*, probably drawn 1420.

clues for the historian of society or technology, an architectural historian may wish to know how a 'traditional' house might have made way for modernist planning, or for the mass production of building parts. The architecture thus becomes evidence of itself, of the decisions and awareness of its designer and/or builder. Is a house exemplary, or symptomatic? Is it important architecturally, or historically?

Architectural historians have tended to enjoy these kinds of ambiguities. Pulling architecture in one disciplinary direction and another means that architecture as a subject sustains perpetual scrutiny from many angles, which in turn feeds back into the knowledge base of architectural historians to the subject's further enrichment. On the question of how to 'do' architectural history, there is no fundamental agreement to be found in and between conferences, universities or any other infrastructure supporting its discussion. This reflects the different patterns through which the knowledge traditions we are about to consider gave modern architectural history a specific scope and structure in each iteration of its appearance.

These observations do not add up to a systematic account of architectural historiography before the emergence of a 'modern' architectural history. They are meant to point, rather, towards a matrix of conceptual and methodological problems inherited by architectural history as it became more clearly differentiated from other modes of historical study from early in the twentieth century. This new field's inheritance from the various strains in which historical knowledge of architecture was understood and transmitted was itself institutionalized, contested and developed. Historiographical issues of influence, style, taxonomy, critical categories (plan, space, form, etc.), progress and change, restoration and preservation, instrumentality, analytical units, the permeability of historical knowledge – these categories shaped the development of architecture's historiography in the first century of academic architectural history. But in doing so, they gave new form to a much longer tradition of finding lessons, trajectories and narratives in architecture's past, and to defining architecture itself in historical terms.

Architectural history as the architect's patrimony

Architectural theory in antiquity

The oldest surviving account of architecture's history was penned in the last decades of the first century BC by Vitruvius, an architect and engineer who, seeking to secure an imperial pension, documented Roman building practices and outlined their general principles. After 2,000 years, we cannot expect much of what Vitruvius understood of architecture to remain relevant to present-day readers. Still, the architect of his *De architectura* understood building materials and their properties, methods of construction, planning and siting, as well as principles of harmonics, heating, sunlight and colour. He understood that architecture relied on 'Order, Arrangement, Eurythmy, Symmetry, Propriety, and Economy'.[3] And he understood that the values of durability, convenience and beauty stood behind worthy buildings.[4] Vitruvius claimed to lay down the rules of architecture as they had been practised up to and during his time to enable Caesar Augustus (most likely) 'to have personal knowledge of the quality both of existing buildings and those which are yet to be constructed'.[5] His ambitions, then, were twofold. First, he sought to explain the formal, semantic and pragmatic dimensions of the buildings of the past. Second, he sought to identify the principles derived from their study that could help architects make good architecture. As he wrote to his Emperor, by understanding the principles that had resulted in superior buildings in Greece and Rome he had become a better judge of architecture in his own time. An architect in the Emperor's service could take Vitruvius' observations and apply them to the conception and construction of new buildings and monuments.

Vitruvius wrote during a transitional phase in the history of Roman architecture, when native principles of architectural composition and engineering governing the form, disposition and decoration of buildings began accommodating a fashion for the architecture of Greece and Asia Minor and from the golden fifth century of the Greek Empire. Vitruvius' treatise is Roman, but it is also a Roman reflection on the historical architecture of Ionian and mainland Greece at a moment in which Romans placed great worth on the art and architecture of that territory, from around the start of the second century BC. Rome knew the architecture of many distant lands, from Spain and Britain to Armenia and Syria, but in the subjugation of Greece, Rome adapted its artful approach to building. Vitruvius' Rome is a hybrid architectural culture: of Rome *and* its territories. Rome welcomed the powerful and permanent influence of Hellenic culture. This did Rome no harm: through respect for and emulation of Greece – the greater historical authority, the originator of artfully building with columns, beams and pediments – Rome's architecture, too, became a worthy exemplar.

From shelter to architecture

De architectura on two occasions describes the origins of the Roman architecture of Vitruvius' day. In the primordial past (book II), people gathered around fire, found a basis for communication and formed communities, which in turn required shelter. The Greeks (book IV) gave order and meaning to the habits and customs of shelter and community, and the authority with which they did so demanded emulation. Their architecture embodied this order, and their architects developed a language for architecture, which the Romans then imitated, adapted and elaborated. On the basis of the Greek model, as presented by Vitruvius, architects skilfully used systems of proportion and decoration to achieve beautiful, fitting and well-disposed buildings.

Consider how Vitruvius presents the three Greek orders (Doric, Ionic and Corinthian) in book IV (1.8). 'Posterity', he writes, found 'pleasure in more slender proportions'. Hence the Doric column is less slender than that of the Ionians (commonly called the Ionic order, but increasingly also the Ionian), and the Corinthian order, which imitates 'the slenderness of a maiden,' is the most fine of all, 'for the outlines and limbs of maidens, being more slender on account of their tender years, admit of prettier effects in the way of adornment'.[6] Early modern treatises regarded Vitruvius' rules as hard and fast. In their study of the extant monuments of antiquity, Sebastiano Serlio (1475–1554) and Andrea Palladio (1508–80) were troubled by the apparent freedom with which Roman architects used the orders: their proportions as much as their decorations. Nevertheless, Vitruvius linked the proportions of the Greek orders to the human body (man, woman and maiden, respectively), which in turn determined their application. The palace of a military officer would, for instance, employ the robust Doric order rather than the delicate Corinthian; the Temples of Vesta, both at Tivoli and in the Foro Romano, employ the Corinthian order rather than the more mature Ionic or the heavy Doric.

3 Sebastiano Serlio, studies of architectural details from the Pantheon, in Book III 'On Antiquities', *Tutte l'opere d'architettura et prospetiva*, 2nd edn, 1544.

Documentation versus advocacy

De architectura illustrates a way of writing about architecture that mixes documentation and advocacy. By imitating this ancient example, architectural treatises written from the fifteenth century onwards assumed this role too. It is difficult to measure, from our present-day perspective, how important Vitruvius' observations or his sometimes heavy-handed rhetoric were in his own time. It seems clear that, from the fall of the Roman Empire until the early phases of what we now call the Renaissance, his treatise was not an important source of instruction about building. When medieval scholars read *De architectura* it was as a classical text, alongside Livy or Plotinus, or for its insights into Roman views on astronomy, astrology and atmospherics. As an architectural history, it offered a model to writers from the fifteenth century onwards. It conveyed knowledge of the past and of the technique of building that made a narrative out of mythical sources and monuments already, in some cases, several centuries old when Vitruvius wrote of them. Vitruvius explained the sources for the art and science of architecture and on their basis described a set of principles and preferences for architecture in the present. Put simply, Vitruvius sought to distil the knowledge of the ancients and transmit this to architects of his own time and of the future.

Leon Battista Alberti's own ten-book treatise on architecture, *De re aedificatoria*, was completed around 1452 during the pontificate of Nicholas V (1447–55). It pursued many of the implications for architecture of its important precursor, Alberti's *De pictura* (1435), a founding theory of painting. In writing on perspective and drawing, Alberti distinguished between the world of bricks and mortar and the intellectual domain of the artistic project, conceived (and executed) on paper by approximating the world through mathematical relationships and drawing. For Alberti, as Rykwert has noted, Vitruvius was less a model for style than for content.[7] As a humanist adept in poetry, philosophy, diplomacy and the law, Alberti addressed the rules of classical architecture as he imagined Cicero might have done had he possessed Vitruvius' technical knowledge. Alberti writes for a contemporary fifteenth-century audience, and although he counts architects among his readers they are not the extent of his public. As an architect himself, Alberti had a secure grasp of architectural technology, which he conveys. The second and fourth books of Vitruvius' treatise assign architecture's origins and development to a socio-cultural process of forming language around technology: social interaction around the fire; the orders around basic shelter. Alberti shifts his theory to position the architect as an agent of social formation and order. On the matter of architecture's origins, therefore, it is telling that Alberti brings to the fore of his work the historical authority on which he writes: 'Since we are to treat of the lineaments of buildings, we shall collect, compare, and extract into our own work all the soundest and most useful advice that our learned ancestors have handed down to us in writing, and whatever principles we ourselves have noted in the very execution of their works.'[8] Alberti draws on the advice and better examples of his forebears, writing a treatise on architecture that is not a direct imitation of his ancient predecessor, but which regards Vitruvius as a paradigm in which Alberti too might work – to different ends and in a different register. This establishes a principle for fifteenth-century relations to the past: as for the treatise, so too for architecture.

An architectural historiography

In making these observations, it is important to recognize that there is no trans-historical, trans-geographical, fixed definition of architecture about which historians can make histories. Much architectural history applies the terms 'architect' and 'architecture' anachronistically, as Pevsner observed in 1942 of the historiography of medieval architecture.[9] Architectural history is always shaped, to one extent or another, by a theory of history and historiography that determines the historical scope and content of architecture as a profession, discipline, art, craft, science or technique. The treatises on architecture written in the fifteenth and sixteenth centuries determined a classical historical canon: a corpus of works to which contemporary buildings could relate conceptually and technically. They also resolved a set of compositional principles building upon the lessons those examples left for the present. These relationships frame architecture as a changing practice with a deep heritage, and the historiography linked to this frame remains deeply embedded in architectural culture. Architecture tends to define itself, through its historians, against historical measures – even when claiming to work beyond history, and even when those measures are made outside of any concept of architecture.

Notwithstanding the suspicious glances (and penetrating stares) to which the great buildings of Western Architecture have, as a canon, been subject in recent decades, together they serve an important function for those architectural histories written first for a professional audience, and which equate history with the patrimony of present-day architectural practice. Such histories do not simply establish the terms under which a past work can offer a precedent, paradigm or model for contemporary architecture. Nor do they necessarily defer to an idea of genealogical continuity among 'families' of architects. More subtly, each history written for architects describes a reservoir of 'architecture' against which is set the scope and terms within which a present-day readership might relate to their intellectual, professional, artistic and technical pasts. By no means must an architectural history look like the historical passages of Vitruvius' *De architectura* or Alberti's *De re aedificatoria* to situate the architect's knowledge and practice in history. Indeed, most writing on the history of architecture does not. As a broad class of histories on which modern architectural historians in particular have built, such historical works establish a strong relationship between the material of their subject and an audience of professionals, commissioning patrons, cultured individuals connected with architectural culture, and so forth. Many an architectural historian has willingly reconciled this relationship with a private sense of artistic and cultural mission.

The architect as artist

Painters, sculptors, architects

In his book *Le Vite dei più eccellenti pittori, scultori ed architettori* (1550, rev. 1568), the painter, architect and biographer Giorgio Vasari drew upon an idea that had survived from antiquity, grouping painters, sculptors and architects as artists and artful artisans.[10] The *Vite* offers the first biographical and historical accounts of the most renowned artists (then, as now) of the Italian Renaissance. It is a founding history of art, but it is also a cornerstone of the intellectual and institutional traditions that have informed architecture's enduring relevance to art historians. Vasari inscribes the buildings of artists and artisans, working as what we now call architects, into the historical canon of Western art. For historians of art and architectural alike, Vasari has continued to shape the historical treatment of the figure of the 'architect-as-artist': the figure whose artistic formation and internal motivations offer insight into their artistic life, which is in turn documented by their art. Works of art carry something of their artist, be this the elusive 'aura' of which Walter Benjamin wrote, the telling details of earlobes and fingernails on which Giovanni Morelli (as Ivan Lermolieff) argued attributions, or formal and semantic structures that the artist shares with others of his or her time.[11] As obsolete as this model for understanding art historically has become, within its parameters we find a series of principles that shaped, to an extent, the early manifestations of what we could think of as a modern architectural historiography, independent from art history, or mostly so.

The artist trope

Vasari's *Vite* offers a way of understanding art and artists that has been repeated time and again since the sixteenth century. It would be obvious that we could find traces of Vasari in Giovanni Pietro Bellori's *Le Vite de' pittori, scultori ed architetti moderni* (1672)[12] or in Alfred Leroy's *La Vie familière et anecdotique des artistes français du moyen-âge à nos jours* (1941).[13] Their titles indicate an allegiance to the genre of artist-biography to which the *Vite* gave rise, even if we can easily understand how they would differ from Vasari's sixteenth-century precedent. Vasari established a writing genre which in turn deployed ancient tropes that have widespread importance for the way we understand the formation and work of artists, and thus of architects *as* artists, even well beyond academic architectural history. These are explored in *Die Legende vom Künstler*, which was first published in 1934 by the Warburg Institute researchers Ernst Kris and Otto Kurz.[14] The book rose to widespread prominence following its translation into English at the end of the 1970s, and offered a way to understand the two-millennia-old literary and rhetorical traditions to which Vasari attended. Kris and Kurz observe that, according to a number of distinct traditions, the artist is often self-educated, copying nature (carving into wood, marking images out in the dirt) while tending livestock (which the artist represents in drawing, imitating nature). The artist is recognized by someone important (another artist, or a nobleman) who can appreciate his skills. These are then cultivated through apprenticeship until they can practise their art independently of the tutors who helped to craft their genius. In Vasari, for example, Raphael serves this role for Giulio Romano. Their cultivation might equally come from a structured independence that allows the artist to make their own way. Vasari presented Lorenzo il Magnifico in this light in his account of the life of Michelangelo.

4   Titian (Tiziano Vecellio), portrait of Giulio Romano, *c.*1536.

For Vasari among members of the Florentine Accademia del Disegno (est. 1562), artistic conception (making art), biological conception (making life from life) and alchemy (transforming matter to a higher state) manifested the same creative process over which artists could claim mastery.[15] Painting, sculpting and designing works of architecture lay somewhere between divine creation and alchemy, between God's hold over the natural world and the powers of the magician. The highest form of art is mimesis, and the architect, as an artist, demonstrates his/her grasp of this power by understanding the workings of mathematics in nature: the rules and relations governing the proportions of plans, façades and ornaments. Command over imitation translates into freedom of invention. This principle is already at stake in the origin stories told by Vitruvius. In Judeo-Christian culture, God is the artist's model, and the artist does a job akin to God himself – in understanding divine systems of proportion the artist can perform such feats as inducing the whole from details, thus the Latin phrase *ex ungue leonem* to describe Phideas' skill in sculpting an entire lion on the basis of its claw alone.[16] So too from the capital of a column might the architect determine the geometrical rules governing the whole building – and then bend them to greater or lesser effect.

If Vasari gave these ancient tropes a literary corollary, he also embedded them in a new historiographical tradition that would dominate writing on architects and other artists through to the nineteenth century. In doing so, he makes this conceptual claim on the architect for art history that has been at the heart of later adaptations of the architect-figure for art historiography. The importance placed on the architect by Vasari and others who wrote histories after the model of his *Vite* raised a number of broad questions for later historians: how does knowledge of an architect's life inform knowledge of his or her work (biographical causality)? To what extent can we find the architect in the work (attribution, authorship)? What is the nature of influence on an artist from his or her institutional or historical settings (contextual causality), upbringing and culture (psychological causality), a 'master' (influence as genealogy), or class, race, gender and sexuality? The special status reserved for the architect by those analysing works of architecture is one of the most persistent dimensions of architectural-history writing.[17] The 'magic' that figure performs is an important dimension of the history of architecture.

An architectural history without names?

To return to those words of Heinrich Wölfflin quoted at the outset, the new aims of academic art history at the end of the nineteenth century add up to a fundamental turn towards the systematic study of art, and of architecture among the arts. This shifted the historian's attention away from the propagation of biographical sketches and artistic anecdotes and the determination of provenance to the almost a-biographical, scientific study of processes of stylistic and formal change and (a generation or so later) to the study of art's meaning and its place in society. All of these changes taking place in art historiography had a direct impact on historians of architecture, many of whom were art historians by training and practice.

A quarter of a century after writing *Renaissance und Barock*, Wölfflin announced in the first edition of his 1915 book *Kunstgeschichtliche Grundbegriffe* his ambition to write a 'Kunstgeschichte ohne Namen' (an 'art history without names'), in which the work of art would exist in history independent of a unique bond with its artist.[18] A painting, sculpture or building would not, first of all, be the work of an artist or architect. A formal reading of any artwork divorced it from biographical circumstances and put into play super-chronological and extra-artistic factors. The history of architectural style and the problem of why the appearance of buildings changes over time assumed new importance in this light. The problem was no longer what Maderno learned from Michelangelo and what Borromini learned from Maderno. Rather the question had become one of how the set of qualities and characteristics of classical Renaissance architecture had been replaced by those of the baroque. (Hence Wölfflin's famous bases of formal comparison, which we will consider below.) Naturally, this intellectual shift occurred in neither an intellectual nor a cultural vacuum. The cultural history pioneered by Jacob Burckhardt in the nineteenth century was crucial in determining these new terms of art historiography. So too were the eighteenth-century developments in philosophy and aesthetics led by the German thinkers Immanuel Kant and Johann Gottfried von Herder.

The reduction of the critical distance of the artwork from the present was a vital aspect of this pivot in modern art historiography from the figure of the artist to the artwork itself. It was achieved by identifying abstract mechanisms and concepts in historical artworks that resonated with their historians and the world in which they wrote. Art survives its artists, and architecture its architects. As long as they continue to do so and remain relevant to a present-day culture, runs this logic, their existence is perpetually contemporary.[19] Writing by Wölfflin and others of his generation explored a balance between investment and critical distance that came to assume fundamental importance for the detachment affected by architectural historiography from the mid twentieth century onwards. Although Wölfflin abandoned the phrase 'Kunstgeschichte ohne Namen' in subsequent editions of *Kunstgeschichtliche Grundbegriffe*, the idea had served to foment a decisive break with a monumental tradition of art history.

Architecture and the history of art

At the end of the nineteenth century, the history of architecture was as subject to changes in art historiography as were the histories of painting and sculpture. Wölfflin read art of the sixteenth and seventeenth centuries across these media, just as Vasari had read the art of the early Renaissance. We ought to appreciate these continuities in the work of late-nineteenth- and early-twentieth-century art historians alongside the novelties that these later historians ushered in. Indeed, the figure of the architect-as-artist remained firmly in play throughout the twentieth century for architectural historians of various backgrounds. For the Italian Stanislao Fraschetti, whose biography of Bernini was published in 1900, a work of architecture evidences the artistic decisions and skills of an individual.[20] Despite its enduring relevance to historical analysis and assessment, the technique of understanding artistic influence, geographical difference, and the tools and tricks of attribution owes much to categories first systematically articulated by Vasari in the sixteenth century. Shaped by formation and circumstance, the architect is measured to varying degrees against both the trope and persona of the artist.[21]

Architecture and empirical knowledge

Architectural history and empiricism

Alongside the historical accounts of architecture found in the treatises by Vitruvius and Alberti, and alongside the artists' lives immortalized by Vasari and those following in his footsteps, the centuries-long process of documenting the premodern architectural remains of ancient and medieval culture offers yet another approach to the problem of knowing architecture historically. Modern architectural historians borrowed from this tradition too. The rise of the empirical sciences from the eighteenth century onwards had widespread repercussions for the way that buildings, sites and monumental sculptures could be known in their own terms, as artefacts. For an archaeologist to document a building or for an architect borrowing the archaeologist's tools of measurement, documentation, analysis and extrapolation, it was not important either to know the identity of the building's architect or builders, or to determine whether or not the building or site qualified as architecture. Archaeology took architecture as a subject of disinterested study based on what could be seen, measured and deduced from the available evidence.

Those who invested in the documentation of ancient buildings and cities were not without motives, be they agents in the expansion of imperial territories or promoters of a higher culture whose model lay somewhere under Egyptian sands or Roman clay. That the tools of their analysis were intended to act against those motives suggests an analogy with the rise of critical philology late in the nineteenth century and on into the twentieth. This manifestation of the elusive quest for a pure knowledge of culture, combined with the growing importance of the empirical foundations of archaeology as a project of documenting the surviving past, set aside the pictures of the ancient world brought alive in the pages of Livy, for example, in order to record truthfully and accurately the remnants of the world he described, which was now underfoot.

From the time of Alberti and the renewed appreciation of Roman antiquity for which he has come to stand, there had been a strong tradition of measuring the extant buildings of the ancient city in order to understand them better as models for contemporary buildings.[22] The new dome of Santa Maria del Fiore in Florence (1418–36) by Filippo Brunelleschi is a famous tribute to the ancient dome of Rome's Pantheon and allegedly relied on his first-hand studies of its structures in the company of Donatello.[23] Architectural treatises regularly presented measurements and scale drawings, advancing through empirical means the task of reinforcing architectural design with principles derived from ancient structures and ruins. Measurement of the work of the past was therefore one process in the refinement of the proportional, formal and semantic systems laid out in prose by Vitruvius and Alberti.

Studying the past

The later distinctions between antiquarian, archaeologist and architect are thus implicated in the studies of antiquity conducted by Serlio, Palladio and Pirro Ligorio (*c*.1510–83). Serlio's *Regole generali di architettura* (1537) was the first book of a projected seven concerning the rules and principles of architecture derived from measurements of ancient examples. His five-volume *Tutte l'opere d'architettura et prospetiva* contained measured drawings and projected views of ancient buildings and monuments (book III), as well as antiquities. Palladio similarly took the ancient architecture of Rome to be the pinnacle of his art's historical achievements and searched out its lessons for his own work. The fourth book of his *Quattro libri* (1570) documents those buildings that remained largely intact, extrapolating what he could deduce from the remaining fragments (sections of walls, columns, etc.) and (book II) demonstrating with examples of his own work those building types that had almost universally been lost to the past, such as residences and other 'minor' types.[24]

Pirro came closest to treating Rome as a site of antiquity in terms aligned with the approaches of early archaeologists. He excavated at the Villa Adriano at Tivoli (from 1549) and drew a map of ancient Rome, the *Anteiquae Urbis Imago* (from 1561), to which the magisterial maps prepared over a century later by Giambattista Nolli (*Nuova pianta di Roma*, 1748) and Giovanni Battista Piranesi (*Campo Marzio dell'Antica Roma*, 1762) were clearly indebted.[25]

The sixteenth-century studies of Serlio, Pirro, Palladio and others maintained a strong sense of Rome's enduring cultural

5   Pirro Ligorio, *Anteiquae Urbis Imago*, 1561, detail.

authority over their time. Whereas these architects measured in order to draw out more delicately the lessons antiquity could offer contemporary architecture, the French scientist and physician Claude Perrault (1613–88) understood that the variation in the measurement of the orders found in Rome's buildings undermined any claim for natural authority that might be made on their behalf. He wrote of 'absolute beauty' and 'customary beauty'. For the former, the difference in relative circumference between one column of the Doric order and another worked against a universal standard for beauty that anyone could appreciate. Architects could negotiate these minor differences between the orders based on their schooling in the classical tradition. In a customary beauty might be found both the regularity of the orders and the possibility of invention within them. For beauty to be available to all on the same terms required that scientific measurement and a law of averages supplant the humanist tolerance for variation negotiated by higher learning. To understand this customary beauty within a tradition meant to understand that it had changed over time.

In his treatise *Ordonnance des cinq espèces de colonnes selon la méthode des Anciens* (1683), Perrault proposed a new system of rules for the architectural orders based on mean measurements of empirically derived proportions, heights, circumferences and other data.[26] His method for studying architectural history was no different from that used to study natural history. He argued against the 'rules' of the Greek and Roman orders. In his hands they became rational systems of disposition, composition and ornamentation. He demonstrated that it was possible to compose classical buildings on an empirical basis. The orders could be invoked independent of the stories of their origin. Their authority was historical, in relation to the known buildings of antiquity, and not based on the mythology to which they supposedly owed their beauty.

Greece versus Rome

Claude Perrault's younger brother Charles perceived the deeper philosophical implications of the problem that his elder brother had explored to great depth in architecture. Written in four volumes between 1688 and 1697, Charles Perrault's *Parallèle des Anciens et des Modernes en ce qui regarde les arts et les sciences* clearly aligned Rome and its humanist apologists with a regressive attachment to 'les anciens'. Greece offered the counter-model of antiquity, behind which fell (modern) France.

This 'dispute' followed an axis running between Paris and Rome. On one side could be found the late-humanist appreciation that antiquity's shadow over contemporary civilization lent life and culture meaning. Rome remained a monolithic idea and, as a constellation of monuments and ruins, it connected the present to a grand past. As the French aristocracy would soon discover, all authority (including that of Rome) had to prove itself consistently worthy. Parisian thinkers presented Greece as a counterweight to Rome. It was an *older* antiquity, a model with deeper roots from which Rome itself had drawn, an advanced society upon which rested 2,000 years of Western culture.

Expeditions to Greece became increasingly feasible from the middle of the eighteenth century as the Ottoman Empire began to stagnate and wane. The French archaeologist Julien-David Le Roy and the British team of James 'Athenian' Stuart and Nicholas Revett published measured drawings of the Greek monuments based on extensive site studies: Le Roy's *Les Ruines des plus beaux monuments de la Grèce* (1758), and the Britons' more expansive four- (later five-) volume study *The Antiquities of Athens* (1762–1816, 1830).[27] The eighteenth century thus witnessed an explosion of knowledge of the former Greek Empire that was called to rally behind 'les modernes'.

Whereas a classical tradition had both risen and been sustained for centuries alongside the architecture of ancient Rome, the buildings and monuments of Greece had been a largely inert presence in the history of architecture – known in literature, but at a remove: an influential corpus known through descriptions rather than by first-hand experience. The Prussian Johann Joachim Winckelmann described Rome's cultural splendour as owing a direct debt to the greater magnificence of the former Greek Empire, publishing *Gedanken über die Nachahmung der griechischen Werke in der Malerei und Bildhauerkunst* in 1755.[28] The connoisseur, collector and antiquarian Pierre-Jean Mariette (1694–1777) also promoted Greece as a modern model of a superior antiquity. The Frenchman identified Rome with the old order of myth, legend and unbounded theocratic authority. Rome spoke to a persistent humanism as Greece spoke to the values of the Enlightenment.[29]

When Piranesi and Mariette went head to head in the 1760s, the issue was hardly limited to whether the architecture of ancient Rome was an 'improvement' on that of Greece, or a 'native', Etruscan invention.[30] Piranesi defended the originality of Rome's contribution to the classical tradition, but in his eyes the findings of the German, French and British archaeologists enjoyed the same footing as the more rhetorical image of Roman antiquity drawn by Nolli (alongside whom Piranesi had worked) and were on a par with the ancient history of Livy (Titus Livius).[31] Piranesi was credentialed as an archaeologist and adept at the dispassionate documentation of ruins, but his views of Rome and the marginalia of his scientific studies belie a perspective that is resolutely antiquarian and humanist. Measurement and myth together give rise to a more powerful historical whole than either could attain on its own.

The facts of the past

The tools brought to bear upon the study of ancient buildings and ruins in the eighteenth century came to have an enduring place among the techniques of architectural historiography. Through observation, measurement and documentation, the extent of an artefact can be surveyed, known independent of its authorship, significance and context. Combining this information with knowledge of building technologies and their history, the stages of a building's construction can be charted and dated with a degree of certainty that has only increased in the last two centuries. The empiricist drive for knowledge for its own sake was not without ideology, as the French historian Michel Foucault reminds us,[32] and the questions of usefulness, application and power are not far behind that of knowledge per se. These questions were largely implicit in the work of the first generations of modern architectural historians, who sought to connect architectural artefacts to aesthetics and thereby undermine empiricism for its own sake. Measurement survived the contingencies of this institutional context to remain a fundamental tool for later historical research in architecture.

Architecture and culture

High culture versus low culture

An a-priori definition of architecture shaped the positions of Palladio and Piranesi on architecture's basic artistic and technical principles, and helped them to navigate the historical authorities on which rested their respective definitions of architecture. The classical tradition made specific reference to the buildings and monuments of Helleno-Roman antiquity. It offered room for invention, though, even if both Palladio and Piranesi actively tested the boundaries of that tradition. Under these terms architectural invention was historically circumscribed. The systematization of knowledge and the flattening out of distinctions between high and low classes of artefacts were together one set of legacies passed in the mid nineteenth century from the empirical sciences to the new *Kulturwissenschaft*, cultural science – or cultural history, as English more commonly has it. This intellectual and institutional development posed a problem for the otherwise elevated art of architecture. The questions and tools of cultural history could now be used to study anything connected to human society: a building as readily as a pair of shoes.[33] The philosophical question concerning architecture's differentiation from other types of building was neutralized by the conceptual position that different kinds of building, or minor architectural details, or stylistic or geographical groupings not traditionally given much weight in the canon, could all nonetheless inform the study of culture and cultural change.

Between the general and the particular

Today, an architectural historian might research and write on the habits of do-it-yourself renovators in the post-war Australian suburbs, or issues of race in New York's public swimming pools. It would not seem necessary to justify why these would fall within the ambit of architectural history, but it would once have been unthinkable to have worked so far beyond the canon.[34] The breadth that characterizes the present-day limits of architecture and its history is but one important legacy of the nineteenth-century cultural sciences.[35] Of the four disciplinary traditions from which academic architectural history emerged as a twentieth-century field, it owes its most direct methodological debts to cultural history. The materials, questions and significance of architectural history research have to one extent or another been informed by its nineteenth-century developments in concert with the knowledge architectural history has drawn from the other traditions introduced above.

In his 1867 architectural history *Die Geschichte der Renaissance in Italien*, Jacob Burckhardt explained the rise of the figure of the architect in terms of cultural mentality and the embedded values of fourteenth- and fifteenth-century mercantile Italian culture.[36] Changes to the status of the individual in Renaissance Italian society – and indeed to society itself – first allowed for the possibility of individual artistic achievements. Thus culture offered a new scale of analysis, subsuming the individual. Burckhardt did not undermine the trope employed by Vasari except to explain the artist in cultural terms. As far as cultural history included the history of art and architecture, it tempered the life and work of the artist as an analytical category, recognizing that, since the sixteenth century, the figure of the artist, as a subject of biography and historiography, had been over-determined by ancient measures and patterns. So too Burckhardt explains the fourteenth-century shift away from theocratic and feudal social structures and their concomitant expression in architecture: 'In the independent cities municipal pride was, above all, to find satisfaction in an imposing cathedral and in outdoing the neighbouring cities. Simple devotion, subject to ups and downs, gave way to state decisions and taxes.'[37] The idea that culture might infuse buildings, paintings or costume, which can in turn be read as expressions of culture, poses two sets of problems for architectural historiography. Firstly, how should architectural historians understand as cultural those artefacts deemed subject to a specific episteme or knowledge system, to be complete in themselves, as art? Or those that operate beyond culture, or claim to do so? Secondly, how might they reconcile the general with the particular, to understand the strength of any given cultural force on the production of a building, a monumental sculpture or an individual architect's works – that is, to see art as cultural expression pure and simple?

Burckhardt gave a new significance and an Italian specificity to the period named by Jules Michelet in the seventh book (1855) of his seventeen-volume *Histoire de France* (1835–67): *La Renaissance*. Writing of architecture among his introductory comments, Michelet cites Brunelleschi's dome of Santa Maria del Fiore as the first instance of a Renaissance architecture, based on reason and mathematics. Of this moment he observes: 'Art finishes, and art begins once more.' The comparatively short-lived 'scholastic age' of the medieval era gave way to rational thought, the rebirth of antiquity, and the discoveries of the world and of man.[38] The concept of rebirth gained institutional traction with *Die Kultur der Renaissance in Italien* (1860),[39] so that when Wölfflin in 1888 came to consider the process of formal change from Renaissance to baroque styles, the Renaissance was well established historiographically. Importantly, Michelet and Burckhardt regarded the Renaissance as a specific gift neither of the arts, nor of rulership, but of culture as an entity and a category in its own right, and known through its manifestations. Renaissance culture therefore formed a substrate for the multivalent Renaissance of the arts: painting, architecture, poetry and so forth.[40] Even when later historians demonstrated the technological and economic underpinnings for the intellectual and artistic developments of the fourteenth and fifteenth centuries, Michelet's broad category of the Renaissance remained the dominant historiographical framework, and the twentieth-century historiography of architecture among the arts continued to address the nature of antiquity's 'rebirth'.

Architecture within the art and cultural sciences

Burckhardt regarded his century as 'better equipped than any other' to study the past. 'As regards the material advantages', he wrote,

> travelling, the learning of languages and the great develop-
> ment of philology have opened up all literatures to our
> modern world; records have become available, travel and
> reproduction, especially photography, have brought monu-
> ments within the reach of everybody, while we have at our
> disposal the vast publication of documents by governments
> and learned societies, which are certainly more open-minded
> and more bent on pure history than was the case with the
> Congregation of St. Maur or Muratori.[41]

History's new ability to treat the past rationally, as 'pure history', was analogous with the nineteenth-century command of science over nature. 'These two branches of learning are alone capable of a detached, disinterested participation in the life of things', Burckhardt observed.[42] It is telling that his most influential considerations of Italian art and culture appear at the same moment as Charles Darwin's *On the Origin of Species* (1859) and Gottfried Semper's *Der Stil* (1860).[43] Along with Burckhardt's *Die Kultur der Renaissance in Italien*, these two books attempt theories of phenomena on a monumental scale: Darwin's of life; Semper's of making; and Burckhardt's of culture. As Burckhardt wisely observed, none would have been possible were it not for advanced cultures of collection and collocation, new reprographic techniques and unprecedented access to parts of the earth once closed or unknown to Europeans and Britons. As for natural science, so too for *Kulturwissenschaft*.[44]

In the later decades of the nineteenth century the academic study of art history, *Kunstwissenschaft*, began to acquire chairs in universities throughout central Europe. Burckhardt himself famously occupied the art history chair in Basel from 1886. The new discipline emerged as a specialization of *Kulturwissenschaft*, a 'scientific' approach to art in distinction from biography and connoisseurship. Art history also owed to the cultural sciences its first generation of academic art historians. In this intellectual setting, architecture was a department of art and the architect a kind of artist. Both, in turn, could be understood culturally using the forms of philological and physical evidence then available. For cultural historians, architecture furthermore traced progress at a scale exceeding the life and works of any individual, and it indexed developments that were extrinsic to the history of architectural ideas as documented in architectural treatises. Architectural history offered a tangible trace of *Zivilisation*.[45]

Burckhardt's work offered a distinction, for instance, between historical source and treatise that underpins the disciplinary detachment necessary for writing architectural history outside the new needs of the nascent architectural profession. He wrote: '[the source] presents the fact pure, so that *we* must see what conclusions are drawn from it, while the treatise anticipates that labour and presents the fact digested'.[46] When his student Wölfflin later set about to write a history of visuality and visual experience, he could read buildings as 'sources' in their own rights. His idea of a 'Kunstgeschichte ohne Namen' rested heavily on Burckhardt's project of reading artefacts at the level of culture. In drawing an analogy between building and costume, Wölfflin asserted that 'the general human condition sets the standard for architecture . . . [A]ny architectural style reflects the *attitude and the movement of people* in the period concerned'.[47] The widely adopted and adapted views on architectural history held by Wölfflin's own students, including Paul Frankl and Sigfried Giedion, in part derive from this understanding of history. Their investment in a spirit of the modernist age, the *Zeitgeist*, is a case in point.

Taken together, the work of these three generations of scholars – from Burckhardt, to Wölfflin, to Frankl and Giedion, as one disciplinary line – grapples with the twin problems of writing architecture into cultural history and writing on architecture in the broader mode of cultural history. Exemplary of this conundrum is the work of Alois Riegl. Among the freedoms Burckhardt had secured was the study of marginal art history (minor works, craft, late style), and Riegl exercised this to profound effect. In his books *Stilfragen* (1893) and *Die spätrömische Kunstindustrie* (1901) Riegl explored the impulse to make art by studying the 'low' artistic categories of ornament and decoration.[48] His 'unit' of this analysis was, in these instances, the *Kunstwollen* (will to make art), rather than the artworks themselves. By understanding how architecture might embody artistic, cultural and psychological phenomena, he set out to understand how changes to architecture over time reflect changes within the deepest strata of culture.

The analytical strategies and conceptual devices of 'classic' cultural history gave rise in the early twentieth century to a range of historiographical approaches to writing on architecture that combined empirical study, philology and intellectual adventurousness. These new approaches served to expand architectural history as a field of study even as they opened specific methods and motivations to sharper criticism.[49]

A modern discipline?

The widespread emergence by the middle of the twentieth century of architectural history as a distinct field of study reflected many decades of institutional and intellectual consolidation. As an academic field, architectural history relied upon the emergence of architecture as a subject of historical, scientific study in the mode of the cultural sciences, informed by architecture's technical specificities and the professional nature of the audience for the books, articles and lectures of architectural historians. Early architectural histories regularly combined the different objectives of, say, biographical knowledge of architects, direct study of their works, and an appreciation of their significance, for both other architects and problems only indirectly connected to architecture. The term 'architectural historian' is almost universally anachronistic when applied to figures working before the mid twentieth century, and even after the Second World War it often ascribes a strong sense of disciplinarity to a way of working better understood as a form of specialization within a parent discipline: in architecture for an art historian; in history for an architect. The roll call for those who position themselves first as architectural historians is rather short, and we should bear this in mind. Whatever the precise disciplinary status of an individual conducting research and writing on the history of architecture, many of those who from the end of the nineteenth century turned to study architectural history outside the traditional terms discussed above cultivated an academic detachment within a humanistic attitude. Whatever shared character we can ascribe to this shift, it remains important to recall that the academic turn to architectural history was largely uncoordinated and polychronic.

A number of individuals born into the German Confederation and Switzerland in the 1850s and 1860s definitively shaped architectural history as a modern discipline or field. The Saxon Cornelius Gurlitt, for instance, chaired the Bund Deutscher Architekten and taught the history of art and of construction at Dresden's Technische Universität. He established the systematic study of the hitherto overlooked architecture of the baroque seventeenth century.[50] Fellow German August Schmarsow taught history of art in Breslau, Göttingen and Berlin, and founded the Kunsthistorisches Institut in Florenz in 1888. His work drew on eighteenth- and nineteenth-century advances in the field of aesthetics in relating questions of space, perception and bodily experience to architecture.[51] Riegl taught art history at the Wiener Universität, where his fellow art historian Franz Wickhoff had been teaching since 1882. Both had studied under Mauritz Thausing and pursued his interest in Giovanni Morelli and his 'scientific', proto-psychoanalytic approach to connoisseurship and attribution.

We opened with the words of Heinrich Wölfflin, whose doctoral dissertation and books pursued the work of Gurlitt and Schmarsow. His first writing threw into relief a series of conceptual questions concerning the way historical architecture might be understood formally and psychologically.[52] A little younger than these other individuals, his impact on architectural historiography of the twentieth century was more persistent, not least because of the later importance of his students. Alongside Gurlitt, Schmarzow, Riegl, Wickhoff and many more others than we can consider here, Wölfflin ushered in a new approach to the study of art and architecture.[53]

As much as these few developments indicate a systematic turn to considering architectural history academically, they hardly point to a consolidated germanophone approach to the subject. Architectural history was, however, treated differently from linguistic community to linguistic community, and within German-speaking architectural historians there could be found as much diversity as among francophone or anglophone historians. There was no single moment in which architectural history, as we might now understand it, went 'on-line'. The emergence of the field was more haphazard and relied on the coincidence of diverse interests across a broad range of geographies.

Outside of German-speaking Europe the magisterial surveys of the British architects Joseph Gwilt (1784–1863), James Fergusson (1808–86) and Banister Flight Fletcher (1866–1953) tracked their Empire's obsession for a critically distant systematization of the world and, in their case, its architecture.[54] History, for them, contained the proper ('true') principles and models for Great Britain, its colonies and its territories. In francophone Europe, France and Belgium drew much from their respective yet interconnected archaeological sciences and architectural heritages, and French architect Eugène Emmanuel Viollet-le-Duc (1814–79) and archaeologist Louis Courajod (1841–96), and Belgian historian Antoine Schayes (1808–56), worked towards understanding artistic and architectural geographies within the broader project of the restoration and conservation of medieval monuments – and around the new problem of national identity to which they were intimately connected.[55] In Italy, a sense of cultural patrimony heightened by its enduring importance to other European cultures drove the work of Italian art historian Adolfo Venturi (1856–1941) and his founding nationalist history of the country's art, *Storia dell'arte italiana* (25 volumes, 1901–40). Across the Atlantic, nineteenth-century American scholars like Benson Lossing (1813–91) and Louisa Caroline Tuthill (1798–1879) were founding an American cultural history and beginning the long process of looking back on Europe with eyes conditioned by cultural proximity and geographical remove.[56]

These very few examples of individuals and groups attending in new ways to the history of architecture during the nineteenth century stand for many more others than we can consider here. Many of these were overtly concerned with describing and understanding the historical architecture and monuments of new or reinvigorated nation-states, kingdoms or empires in light of a project of cultural advancement tied to what Burckhardt and Michelet had called the 'Renaissance' or its 'natural' Romantic counter-example, bound to the architecture of the middle ages. That moments of 'crisis' and 'decline' would offer compelling subjects for some of these historians suggests that those who celebrated the rise of advanced cultures in the past also understood their impermanence.

Many of the tenets of an art history of architecture, and of an architectural history written by and for the architecture profession, were teased out over the course of the nineteenth century. It remained for a generation of scholars and architects born in and around the 1880s, whose intellectual formation almost uniformly precedes the outbreak of the First World War, to firmly establish the conditions, tools and objectives of architectural historiography as we recognize it today. This work together comprises the modern architectural history that Wölfflin and his generation helped to set in train.

A close encounter with the English scholars Geoffrey Scott and Martin Briggs from around the First World War onwards makes clear the debts these owe to Wölfflin and Gurlitt, as well as the important function performed by both in disseminating and popularizing their perspectives on architecture's history to a widely dispersed anglophone readership. In a similar manner, the French art historian Henri Focillon (1881–1943, later an influential professor at Yale University) developed a long-standing engagement with the German-language discussions on space, perception and change.[57] Louis Hautecœur likewise confronted questions of periodization, style and the systematization of cultural artefacts. Hautecœur's (originally) seven-volume *Histoire de l'architecture classique en France* (1948–57) echoes Venturi's Italian project of decades earlier while offering its own important advances.[58] Venturi's former student Gustavo Giovannoni (1873–1947), an architect and art historian, mobilized his historical knowledge to practical ends by addressing the close relationship of architectural form to urban form in respect of Italy's proliferation of monumental heritage. Giovannoni grappled with the issue of producing architecture in a setting replete with reminders of the past's endurance, balancing client needs with the important task of assessing and preserving buildings and monuments of the past.

Whereas for Wölfflin and Scott the shift from Renaissance to baroque styles was of key importance, Focillon saw parallel themes in medieval cathedrals and the recurring 'life' of artistic forms. The German art historian Wilhelm Worringer, in his important volume *Abstraktion und Einfühlung* (1907) likewise argued for super-geographical and super-chronological phenomena that could be identified according to critical and architectural themes.[59] So too did Frankl, who married questions of space and perception in medieval architecture with the classical tradition that appeared in the early modern period in Italy and elsewhere. Frankl, Worringer and Focillon made important claims, each according to their own terms, on medieval architecture that expanded the remit of critical categories and historical patterns previously understood as largely the domain of the classical tradition. Wölfflin's other famous disciple, Giedion, perceived the development across history of what he saw as fundamental constants in architecture, most notably 'space', which he regarded as predicated in the architecture of the ancients and fulfilled in the work of modernist architects in the mid twentieth century. Giedion's work formed a mould for one of the most widely resonating themes of twentieth-century architectural history.

In a variety of ways, and in a number of places, these generations of scholars exposed architectural history to a new kind of scrutiny, which continues to resonate with present-day work in the field.

2
Organizing the past

Given the diverse intellectual and institutional origins of modern academic architectural history, it is hardly surprising that contemporary architectural historians would approach the task of analysing the past from any of a number of different perspectives. This chapter surveys some common strategies for considering architecture historically. Each evidences a form of (usually benign) historicism, a conception of the past's relation to the present, and thus of the present's historicity. Herder invoked this consciousness when he wrote, 'A slender thread connects the human race, which is at every moment breaking, to be tied anew.'[1] The division of architectural history by a chronology governed by style and period is one of the earliest, more traditional and most persistent approaches to this problem. The problems of defining specific styles and understanding the transitions that occur between one style and another (gothic to Renaissance; Renaissance to baroque) constitute the first disciplinary problems of architectural history. For these reasons we will consider it first, and in slightly greater length than other approaches.

During the nineteenth century, the confluence of stylistic, cultural, social and historical factors in the composition of contemporary buildings prompted architects and historians alike to align architectural styles, including proportional and ornamental systems, with their historical origins, which in turn bore a set of values. When a building could be designed in the manner of a historical style – classical, byzantine, baroque and so forth – the historian's question of how to define a style assumed a greater importance for the theory and practice of architects. 'In welchem Style sollen wir bauen?' asked Heinrich Hübsch in 1828: 'In what style should we build?' Hübsch's essay provoked a debate on the theme among German architects and academics of his time, during an era in which, to quote one of his respondents, architects could be found working 'in every style or none'.[2]

A more pragmatic discussion on this same set of issues could be found centred on Cambridge around this time – echoing countless others elsewhere. Members of the Cambridge Camden Society (established 1839) held strong views on the appropriate style for Anglican churches in Britain's new colonies and territories. Writing in their journal *Ecclesiologist*, George Selwyn, Bishop of New Zealand, in 1841 advised that 'Norman is the style adopted; because as the work will chiefly be done by native artists, it seems natural to teach them first that style which first appeared in our own country.'[3] For the nineteenth century, when stylistic decisions no longer seemed given, much thought was dedicated to determining the most appropriate appearance for a building in any specific setting. Where German architects appreciated the problem faced by their nineteenth-century contemporaries as concerning the choice of style among a relatively free range of options, the Cambridge Camden Society saw a more natural logic to the selection of a style appropriate to a place relative to the pace of its religious, artistic and technical progress.

The histories of architectural style that appeared in the nineteenth century thus contended with two kinds of problems. How, on one hand, could the past be known and represented? And how, on the other, could those architectural styles embodying recognizable values be taken up or set aside within a long process of cultural assessment and assimilation? As we shall shortly see, stylistic histories of architecture contributed to the nineteenth century's larger cultural projects of knowing the world in its entirety (witness the world exhibitions, encyclopedias) and constructing taxonomies of all things, from insects, fish and the chemical elements to culture and its multiform expressions.[4] Likewise, questions of style and stylistic transformation were fundamental to the disciplinary toolkit and cultural ambitions of architectural historians working at the end of the nineteenth century and thus steered, at least initially, the nascent academic field of architectural history.

Approach

The following pages consider a number of ways in which architectural historians have, from the later decades of the nineteenth century, addressed the task of writing about the past. We might think of this as an issue of method. Where methodological differences between one historian and another can seem marked in early cases, however, they tend to be more ameliorated in recent histories of architecture, to the extent that it is often unproductive to apply a methodological schema to the field of architectural history, or to understand the work of an architectural historian purely on methodological grounds. We might speak instead of methodological biases or allegiances, but these will rarely be doctrinaire.

The softer term 'approach' is therefore useful for attending to the various ways in which historians of architecture address the question of architectural history's 'unit', while acknowledging that an individual will often use combinations of frame, material and method that best suit the subject of a historical study. The term 'unit' here refers to the way the historian divides into workable portions the 'total history' of architecture – the hypothetical but obviously impossible complete past of everything that has happened everywhere at all times as it can be understood from all perspectives. The question of the historian's approach can also help us to appreciate how he or she deals with the management of architectural history's apparent demand for infinite relativism, whereby all knowledge depends on the point of view from which it is generated and represented.

Aside from numerous anthologies that set out to group essays and extracts from books into methodological or theoretical categories, a number of monographic studies, mainly concerning art history rather than architectural history, will shed further light on the points raised throughout this chapter.[5]

Mark Roskill's *What is Art History?* (1976) works through a series of conceptual and methodological themes, sticking close to the history of painting, but making a number of points of interest to a discussion on methods of architectural historiography.[6] The *Research Guide to the History of Western Art*, by W. Eugene Kleinbauer and Thomas P. Slavens (1982), makes many pertinent observations on style, period and transition, as well as on interpretative frameworks.[7] Again their subject is the history of art, but the methodological issues and examples they raise often parallel or overlap with those found in architectural history. Laurie Schneider Adams's well-organized survey *The Methodologies of Art* includes discussion and examples of a range of media and positions on art-historical method.[8] Likewise, Michael Podro's *The Critical Historians of Art* (1982) is an astute biographically arranged study of perspectives and approaches. His book also principally concerns art historians, but many of these, as we have considered above, wrote on architecture and also fall in the remit of our interests.[9] In his book *Methodisches zur kunsthistorischen Praxis* (1977), Otto Pächt works across artistic media, including architecture, to offer a personal but privileged insight into methodological problems shared by historians of art and architecture.[10]

In this chapter we consider six approaches to the organization of the past of architectural history: style and period, biography, geography and culture, type, technique, and theme and analogy. An architectural historian would not tend to follow one of these modes exclusively. As such, these headings are much less a methodological map of the field of architectural history than a limited survey of historiographical approaches, where one is often tempered through its combination with others.

Style and period

In an essay called 'Style', first published in 1962, James Ackerman observed that 'for history to be written at all we must find in what we study factors that are at once consistent enough to be distinguishable and changeable enough to have a "story"'.[11] For the historian of art and architecture, 'works . . . are the primary data; in them we must find certain characteristics that are more or less stable'. Style, he writes, is a 'distinguishable ensemble of such characteristics'.[12] Works of art, and works of architecture among them, are rarely preserved for their intrinsic artistic merit. This means that the facts and circumstances of a building's conception and realization are susceptible to loss over time. The intentions, formation and even the identity of the artist, architect or mason can be obscured, or disappear entirely. In these circumstances especially, 'style is an indispensable historical tool; it is more essential to the history of art than to any other historical discipline'.[13] Nevertheless, style is a structure applied by historians to history rather than a logic extracted from the past. The question the historian must ask, Ackerman notes, is 'what definition of style provides the most useful structure for the history of art?'[14]

When Heinrich Wölfflin, writing half a century earlier, posed the possibility of conceiving of an 'art history without names', he too proposed that one could understand architecture's history on the basis of its appearance and visual character and the changes to which they were subject over time. Ackerman's reflections on style soften the sometimes-hard formalism of Wölfflin's approach, rendering style useful as an analytical category without requiring adherence to a doctrine. For both historians of architecture the evidence for a stylistic history would be the building itself. The stylistic makeup would include decoration, details and the visual organization of the building's façade given by the architectural order used in its columnation, or its form and massing. How does a building balance stability and change within history? Why do styles change over time? How can we know one style from another? How can we name stylistic periods, and understand how they rise and fall, when architecture as a category of the arts is made up of individual works?

Wölfflin belonged to the first generation of those who sought to systematise historical knowledge of architecture among the arts. In *Kunstgeschichtliche Grundbegriffe* he lent analytical criteria to stylistic divisions based on a comparative method of visual analysis, observing that styles followed a cyclical path from nascent, to classic, to baroque states. The nascent state held the promise of the classic, just as the baroque traced its deterioration. The question embedded in the introduction of *Renaissance und Barock* follows this logic: how did we go from Raphael and Michelangelo to Maderno and Borromini in a few short decades? For Wölfflin, 'baroque' is a stylistic epithet coloured by its derogatory heritage, denoting that which is overwrought and super-exuberant, just as 'Renaissance' takes on the celebratory tone given it by Burckhardt – the rebirth of an ancient model, sure of its principles and close to a beautiful ideal.

Wölfflin's *Kunstgeschichtliche Grundbegriffe* goes much further than this judgement by codifying the methods for the kind of formalist analysis on which his own histories rest.[15] He lays out a set of now well-known dichotomies to explain the differences between classical and baroque buildings, paintings and sculpture: linear versus painterly, plane versus recession, closed versus open form, multiplicity versus unity, and clearness versus unclearness. Wölfflin's own lectures at the universities of Basel, Berlin and Zurich followed this comparative technique. He would show two slides at once in order to describe and explain the differences between one building and another, and hence between one stylistic category and another. Until the advent of digital projection, the paired display of slides was a common tool for teaching the history of art and architecture. It was initially bound to the formalist, rather than iconological, teaching of architectural history, but was later widely adopted by many teachers who paid little heed to its original methodological connotations.

For Wölfflin, style concerns deep structure as well as appearance. It is the device by which we can tell one architect or writer apart from others, but also families and generations of buildings. Just as in speech, writing and dress, we can with variable levels of confidence tell the difference between products of the seventeenth century and those of the nineteenth, between those of the twelfth and of the fifteenth. It is this concept of style of which Peter Gay wrote in 1974 (of styles of history-writing):

Style is the pattern in the carpet – the unambiguous indication, to the informed collector, of place and time of origin. It is also the marking on the wings of the butterfly – the unmistakable signature, to the alert lepidopterist, of its species. And it is the involuntary gesture of the witness in the dock – the infallible sign, to the observant lawyer, of concealed evidence. To unriddle the style, therefore, is to unriddle the man.[16]

Between Ackerman and Wölfflin, then, we have two different approaches to understanding style historically, each with connotations for the writing of history. Wölfflin maintains the idea that style is a visual revelation of the state of a work, which is a product (and therefore an index) of its time. The historian can understand a culture by understanding its art. The periodic division of historical time follows this logic, whereby the Renaissance, for example, is first a social, political and economic development, and secondarily a development in the arts. As we might expect to find with the passage of decades, Ackerman's position ameliorates Wölfflin's and comes closer to a flexible working definition of style.

The word *style* defines a certain currency – distinguishable in the work (or in some portion of the work) of an artist, a place, or a time – and it is inefficient to use it also to define the unique traits of single works of art; uniqueness and currency are incompatible. The virtue of the concept of style is that by defining *relationships* it makes various kinds of order out of what otherwise would be a vast continuum of self-sufficient objects.[17]

Many art and architectural historians of the last century found style a useful 'protection against chaos'.[18] In his guide, *L'Art de reconnaître les styles*, written around 1900, Émile Bayard considers style across architecture, decoration, monuments and (principally for him) furniture.[19] Style, he suggests, is fundamentally physiognomic, and, for architecture and furnishings as for animals and vegetables, one can trace developments of new species and within species, each responding to the constraints of 'nature' and the inclination to 'progress'. We can appreciate, of course, how the analogy of 'recognizing' styles as one recognizes the features of an individual in relation to categories is a product of nineteenth-century thinking in the natural sciences. It relies on a capacity for a rigorous taxonomy that most historians of architecture can no longer countenance, but which was an important aspect of stylistic architectural historiography in the first part of the twentieth century. This followed the nineteenth-century examples, especially, of Fergusson and Fletcher, and was manifest, for instance, in the global survey (from antiquity to the middle ages) of François Benoit.[20]

It is not enough to understand that with stylistic labels come fixed rules pertaining to proportion, decoration, colour or any other factor governing a building's appearance. Whereas many have soundly rejected the notion of a stylistic system for the history of architecture, it has often been replaced awkwardly by chronological groupings that serve as stylistic epithets in disguise. Other debates have circled around the propriety of using stylistic and periodic terms that were later applied to historical phenomena as unifying devices (Romanesque, gothic, rococo) alongside stylistic labels under which architects grouped themselves contemporaneously (International Style, postmodernism, deconstructivism). Where one lends order to chaos, to again recall Ackerman's phrase, the other manipulates the techniques of historians to historicize architecture as it is being made, and in these examples facilitate its entrance to the museum. This latter approach sets out tenets against which individual examples can be tested, and within which subsidiary groupings will appear. Dutch International Style can be distinguished from North American by the expert, as can that of California from that of New England. Progressive historians and theoreticians of architecture might treat postmodern historicism as conservative while ascribing to formal postmodernism and the neo-avant-garde the progressive tones of modernism.[21]

These examples are deliberately blunt and can be easily contradicted so as to expose the inevitable fallacies faced by schemes that set out to organize the history of architecture according to appearance. Any stylistic or periodic organization of past buildings and monuments will introduce the problems of reconciling the individual example with a normative rule against which very few cases can be measured without compromising either the single building or the norm against which it is measured. Where a label offers a useful visual trigger for the historian, it would these days be treated with a healthy dollop of scepticism, and, when deployed, viewed as a 'soft' rule, recognizing exceptions as being more than failed attempts to fulfil a perfect model. The relatively recent appearance of the stylistic term 'Renaissance Gothic' is a good example of historians recognizing the inadequacy of monolithic stylistic–periodic terms to describe historical examples.[22]

On this point we ought to turn briefly to one application of stylistic divisions in architectural historiography, namely, the process of arguing the representative character of a building in legal cases concerning architectural heritage, especially

6   Renaissance Gothic: Stephan Weyrer the Elder, Church of St George, Nördlingen, nave and choir vaults, *c*.1500.

of the last two centuries. To what extent is the building at hand exemplary of Federation Style or of Georgian or of Neo-classical or of Modernism? Note the capital letters, denoting hard definitions of these styles. For the architectural historian giving evidence, this kind of assessment would seem outdated, but it has strong traction outside of the academic study of architectural history and remains a useful tool in the classification and protection of architectural heritage on formalist or aesthetic grounds.[23]

The formalist and taxonomic approaches to style that marked the work of architectural historians in the nineteenth and early twentieth centuries have had a more productive afterlife than the staid identification of styles and periods, in many cases opening the work of architecture and its history to questions of philosophy and the deeper structures of culture. They have also allowed historians of architecture to pursue the relation of architecture to the visual arts (principally painting and sculpture) on chronological grounds other than biography, which we shall consider next. This connects artistic production to time and raises the loaded question of the degree to which time lends the architect the constraints of their practice. Do technology, religion, social mores, taste, economics and other external factors shape architecture's appearance and inform its capacity to change, or does architecture govern its own formal laws according to its own body of theory? This question remains open to debate.

Those architectural historians who accepted Arnold Hauser's invitation (1959) to write a 'Kunstgeschichte ohne Namen' based on the measure of society rather than style accepted that architecture's appearance could be informed by factors completely external to the artistic workings of architecture and its traditions.[24] The classicism of the Renaissance manifests the new economic, religious and political conditions of the fourteenth and fifteenth centuries on the Italian peninsula. To take Renaissance architecture as a unit of analysis is not, therefore, to accept the stylistic unity of this architecture as a purely architectural phenomenon. From this point of view, it is rather to regard this architecture as evidence of historical forces unified by factors that remain relatively constant across the period marked by the emergence of a market economy from a feudal society, until to the Sack of Rome and the religious wars heralded another fundamental shift in the bases of society and culture.

The architectural histories of this period by Charles Burroughs, Manfredo Tafuri and Deborah Howard all engage the problem of architecture's subjection to extra-artistic forces, but they do so within the traditions of cultural history, treating the Renaissance as a cohesive historical epoch containing the full range of its expressions.[25] This division of architectural history according to major historical events and the various degrees of historical cohesion they allow historians to address is a legacy of the cultural histories of Michelet and Burckhardt. It accepts that architecture is a manifestation of culture, and therefore a form of historical evidence – traces of historical forces that are evidenced, too, by a range of cultural and social phenomena.

The bifurcation of historiographical positions during the 1950s and 1960s on the meaning of mannerism in sixteenth-century Italian art and architecture highlights a key difference between internal and external criteria for the cohesion of historical periods.[26] Mannerism is itself a contentious term. Among those historians for whom it had some valency, however, some understood mannerism as an artistic, linguistic deformation within the classical tradition, while others positioned it as an expression of the uncertainties of the age, of the loss of surety and the universal values of the Roman church. One historiographical value (invention) is architectural and artistic; another (anxiety) is cultural, societal and religious. Particularly in more recent decades, architectural historians have shifted from the treatment of 'internal' historiographical categories of past epochs: the Roman Empire, the middle ages, the Renaissance, the Counter-Reformation, the modern world since the Industrial Revolution. The architectural history of politico-cultural periods, indicated in such epithets as Weimar Germany, New Deal America, Fascist Italy, Colonial Brazil, Soviet Russia, post-war Japan and so forth, take architecture as a trace of events and agendas that are not its own, but which nevertheless implicate its historical development.

The division of history by style and period is not, therefore, a monolithic approach, even if it has enjoyed a sustained role in organizing the history of architecture. Style and period open a door on the question of the extent to which architecture's internal artistic forces balance those that shape it from the outside. Conceptually, style and period have some fundamental differences, but as categories that allow the architectural historian to begin arranging the drawings, buildings and ruins of the past they share an abstract approach to historical time based on variable unities within definable parameters. This returns us to Gay's definition of style and the problem it has posed for historians of architecture. If style is, indeed, the pattern in the carpet, the markings on the wings of the butterfly, and the gesture of the witness in a court case, then the problem this leaves the historian of architecture is how to account for the origins of these patterns, marks and gestures. When they occur within the history of architecture, are they architectural in nature, or historical?

Biography

As we saw in the first chapter of this book, the tradition of writing biographical portraits of artists, including some figures we now identify as architects, offered one important model for an academic architectural history as it emerged at the end of the nineteenth century. This tradition indexed examples like Antonio di Tuccio Manetti's biography (*c.*1480) of Brunelleschi and Vasari's sixteenth-century *Vite*.[27] It equated architectural history with the history of architects. However far contemporary architectural histories concerned with the architect might have moved from Vasari's mode of writing history, they still owe to him the fundamental division of time according to lifespan, its trajectory and works, and its repercussions and relations with other biographical entities. The life-and-works genre of architectural history is a persistent way of accounting for the contributions of the individual to history.

We could spend a great deal of time on its mechanisms alone. The observations that follow, however, also pertain to a biographical organization of architectural history concerned with corporate entities and the activities of patrons, like emperors, popes and presidents. Architectural histories that plot the origins, intentions, influences and impact of a government or institution can likewise assume some of the characteristics of a biographical architectural history. Indeed, a building, or a city, can be said to have its own life, and the terms and structures of biography can inflect its histories: foundations, rise to prominence, height of influence or importance, and dénouement – literary strategies, indeed, dramatic even, but shared with biography nevertheless. The kind of architectural history with which this section is concerned is, therefore, an architectural history organized in relation to an entity that either is biological or sustains a biological analogy. Because the history of architecture has enjoyed a long and close association with the figure of the architect, we will focus our attention on the organization of historical time according to the life of the individual architect: the biographical architectural monograph as a genre of architectural history.

This kind of history treats architecture as evidence of the architect's actions and intentions. From this perspective, one architect's lifework connects to another's by means of his or her formation, motives, influences (exerted by or on the subject), settings, opportunities and, more loosely, professional and artistic genealogies. This approach has in recent decades also allowed for the psycho-biographical interpretation of historical subjects. However a life is constituted historically, and however the historian might deal with the content of that life, a subject's birth and death lend firm starting and finishing points to any given subject. (Against this observation one might substitute a partnership's establishment and dissolution; or a government's rise and demise.) These often determine the most immediate associations of a lifework to a period, style, type, geography and so on. They can also inform the way that one individual subject relates to another, or that subjects relate to the numerous contexts that shape or colour historical events. The facts and conditions of an architect's birth and death lend architectural history an order determined by biographical progression – of the stages of life, and of the relationship of the architect as an individual and the external forces acting upon him or her.[28]

It is important to recognize that biography is inevitably, to a greater or lesser extent, a construction of its author. The historical treatment of biographical subjects will be informed by the historiographical trends of the time in which the work is written as it seeks to present what is known and can be known (and is relevant to know) of the individual concerned. Many major figures of the architectural canon furthermore index broader historical developments in architecture: Brunelleschi for the Renaissance, Borromini for the baroque, Thomas Jefferson for the Enlightenment, Le Corbusier for modernism, and so forth. To invoke one or other of these names is to recall the entire baggage of this association and the historical discourse that has already accrued around it.

Architectural history organized along biographical (and occasionally autobiographical) lines most commonly includes monographs, as well as the *œuvre complète*, which present a known body of an architect's work and establish frameworks for its analysis. This is a favourite curatorial mode of the museum, because the facts of a person's life can often be made to lend neat divisions for the interpretation of the subject's work. These might include major life events, travel and migration, realization (or not) of significant works, and so forth. Even if those divisions can be called to account by an exhibition's critics, a knowing reviewer or other literature in the field, they regularly establish a basic chronology and organizing structure.

A biographical organization of architecture's history relies on a concept of architecture as an authored work, and of the architect as an artist or craftsman – an active agent in the work. This idea is relatively recent, enjoying continuity only since the Renaissance. Even when architectural history makes a claim on the city, it is feasible to name 'authors' against whom one can measure the unfolding of an intentioned plan, such as Albert Speer for the Third Reich's Berlin, Robert Moses for modern New York, Ernst May for *Das Neue Frankfurt*, and – citing more obvious examples that evidence a heavier individual hand – Walter Burley and Marilyn Mahoney Griffin for Canberra, Le Corbusier and Pierre Jeanneret for Chandigarh, and Lucio Costa for Brasilia. In these instances, the plan can be understood to have the autonomy of an architectural work in order that it can be considered in light of the architect's œuvre.

Two major exhibitions on Ludwig Mies van der Rohe (1886–1969) were staged concurrently in New York in 2001: *Mies in Berlin* at the Museum of Modern Art, and *Mies in America* at the Whitney Museum of American Art.[29] Together they illustrate some of the points raised above. Here the architect's work is organized along the clear division of his European and American 'periods', divisible by his 1937 emigration from Germany. How does Mies's work change after his move to Chicago? What aspects of his work 'belong' to Berlin? And what property belongs to the US? What among his work and ideas transcend the place of his practice – or the intellectual and artistic context of the modern movement, for which he is customarily claimed? The trajectory of this story can be cast long – from earliest influences on the young Mies to his posthumous influence on others – or short – from the first building to the last. The bio-geographical division maintained by the two museums and curatorial teams (led by Terence Riley and Barry Bergdoll at the Museum of Modern Art and Phyllis Lambert at the Whitney) suggests a large subsidiary unit of 'the life' within which Mies historians find smaller sets of his architectural projects.

7   Mies and America? Jacqueline Kennedy chatting with Ludwig Mies van der Rohe, 12 April 1964, Hyannis Port, Mass.

Biographical architectural history raises a number of specific conceptual issues. The reasons for any biographical turn can be given as hard or soft, evidencing direct causality or the subtle influence of any number of circumstantial factors working together. An architect's lifework might give rise to persistent themes, which take on the appearance of an intellectual or artistic project that demands interpretation as much as it defies it, or that justifies aligning the architect with others who appear to share his or her professional and artistic concerns. The degree to which a specific building, suburban plan, monument or unrealized design can be wholly explained by the architect's enduring artistic, cultural or technological project; by the architect's personality; by the cultural, historical and geographical circumstances of his or her life; or even by the explanations he or she might give for the work at hand: each is open to criticism by those who would put the external forces of economics, politics, religion, materials, building technology, intellectual formation and professional institutions into play as forces stronger than any one architect's will.

Many architectural histories written in the biographical mode are openly hagiographic and set out to install an architect in the canon or to defend his or her place there. Many architects themselves have not proven averse to writing historical accounts of their own lives and practices, with the effects ranging from critical to advertorial. Even the most obviously biased and blinkered studies of individual architects can, however, serve the valuable function of documenting the relevant facts and sources relating to someone's life in practice. Those books and exhibitions produced with the aim of introducing an architect to the world are often works of passion and dedication that are a fundamental foundation of materials upon which a later historian can build as he or she works back over the subject. Subsequent research will inevitably uncover new materials, revise chronologies and reassess the significance of individual projects. That does not diminish the importance of the first step of recording the architect's life and work. Indeed, much of what we call 'critical architectural history' relies on this initial, often uneven layer of research and analysis.

Other architectural histories openly seek to strike a balance between intrinsic and external forces acting on the architect's work, even if this results in a more 'realistic' (or compromised) portrait. The volumes organized and introduced by Marco De Michelis on *Heinrich Tessenow, 1876–1950* (1993) and Johan Lagae on Claude Laurens (2001) tread this line to great effect.[30] Each follows the rules of an *œuvre complète*, reflecting on the various meanings that one might impose on the biographical subject, between free agent and index. Like the books on Mies van der Rohe introduced earlier, they nevertheless treat their respective architects critically as well as historically, testing their work against themes and comparative cases that hold their subject accountable to the broader histories in which they take part, all the while retaining the clear limits imposed by life's boundaries and trajectories.

Geography and culture

The characteristics of an architectural history shaped by biographical factors parallel those borrowing limits from national, imperial, regional, municipal and other geo-political borders, or those that map onto cultural and/or linguistic territories, extra-territorial groupings and geographies, or diasporas. The architectural history of a nation can be studied as a discrete field of knowledge, despite the obvious complications and compromises that inevitably arise from modern nations sharing borders that have been subject to varying degrees of permeability, or that are introduced by immigration and emigration. The architectural history of a contemporary nation, for example, might include formerly discrete territories, or discernible linguistic regions whose architectural history has developed coherently within a larger nationalist grouping. A twentieth-century nation might be subject to the mechanisms of colonization, connecting one territory and its history with that of the colonial party, and ultimately to its other colonies. The architectural histories of South Africa, Australia, New Zealand and Canada are distinct on any number of terms while sharing the colonial experience under British rule.[31] So too for South Africa, Indonesia and New York in relation to Dutch colonization. Few historians of architecture would regard the concept of nation or territory to be so straightforward and passive as the lines of a map suggest. This is not to say that these lines do not offer a useful starting point for considering the architecture of a territory or culture.[32]

A history of Swiss architecture, to give one example, might be resolutely introspect or openly treat the problems, both practical and conceptual, of architects moving easily between one country and another, originating in Switzerland or moving there, or identifying strongly with one neighbour or linguistic community. A curious example of a history contending with this kind of geographical permeability is the American G. E. Kidder Smith's modernist history and photographic survey *Switzerland Builds: Its Native and Modern Architecture* (1950). In a long preface, the Prague-born Swiss historian Sigfried Giedion offers a distracted reflection on the 'character' of the Swiss, which is extended in the content of Smith's account. Giedion's 'Introduction to Native Architecture' begins with this explanation:

> The native, or vernacular, building shown on the following pages is comprised of the dwellings in which the people of the country live, and the buildings which they use in gaining their livelihood, such as barns and agricultural adjuncts. The book will not deal, except in passing, with the richer communal monuments or public buildings of derivative 'styles' – largely foreign – for these, even in remote districts, were almost always done under the patronage or influence of the church or local government, both of which were well versed in architectural developments abroad. Churches will be touched upon because they are so intimately tied up with the lives of the inhabitants, but not the cathedrals, nor the Renaissance, Gothic or Baroque as such. These forms can be seen in far finer examples in the countries of their origin on the four sides of Switzerland.[33]

The qualification for being included in *Switzerland Builds* is the demonstration of a native character. For Giedion this excludes those works of Swiss architecture that adopt and adapt styles, forms and types that originate elsewhere and thus speak to (for instance) the history of ecclesiastical architecture in Europe.

Published almost twenty years later, *New Directions in Swiss Architecture* (1969) is a book of comparable scope and intention. Its authors Jul Bachmann and Stanislaus von Moos take a more ambivalent stance to Smith's qualification of autochthonous character. Although the country can lay claim to some clear identifications, namely 'machines, chocolate, cheese, and watches, and beyond its famous "neutrality"', they ask 'is there any value which could be defined as specifically Swiss?'[34] The scope of Bachmann and von Moos's book is close to that of Smith's. Both concern modern architecture, but whereas the latter example seeks out that work demonstrating a real affinity with the place, the former considers the function of the territory as a setting for exchanges that work between Swissness and European internationalism.

At the risk of spending too long on this one national example, a third book, roughly contemporaneous with the previous two, illustrates one further stance available to historians concerned with the limits offered by geo-political borders. Eberhard Hempel introduces his authoritative contribution to Pevsner's 'Pelican History of Art' series, *Baroque Art and Architecture in Central Europe* (1965), with a series of historical and conceptual observations.[35] These concern economics, arts and letters, religion, the organization of arts practices, and patronage and style, before undertaking studies bordered on one side by territory and on the other by chronology. Hempel divides his book chronologically, with his history concerning (to cite his subtitles) *Painting and Sculpture: Seventeenth and Eighteenth Centuries* and *Architecture: Sixteenth to Eighteenth Centuries*.

Curiously, Hempel treats political territories as mobile categories in relation to the broader subjects of the book (architecture, painting and sculpture). Therefore, in the sections entitled 'The Heroic Age, 1600–39' and 'The Years of Recovery after the Thirty Years War, 1640–82', territorial cases fall under the heading 'Architecture' – Austria, Hungary, Bohemia and Moravia, etc., and Switzerland also. The two subsequent sections, entitled 'The Baroque Period, 1683–1739' and 'Rococo and its End, 1740–80', take their headings from these territories, which are then further divided up to three times: into 'Architecture', 'Sculpture' and 'Painting'. Some miss a category. Prussia is considered for its contribution to the baroque period, while Silesia's rococo arts rate merely a passing mention.

Switzerland participates in broader artistic and historical phenomena shared by Austria, Hungary and Poland, for instance, but lends to these broad developments grouped under the broader geography of Central Europe a cultural, historical, geographical and technical specificity that must (for Hempel) be balanced out with the general history of this period.

The depth of histories framed on geo-political grounds is also determined by the histories of the borders themselves. Hempel's history of Central European baroque reconciles contemporary (for 1965) nations with former territories. The former state of Czechoslovakia, therefore, appears among his subheadings, but so do Bohemia, Moravia and Silesia, which formed part of that state from 1918 to 1993, and part of the Czech Republic to the present. Looking farther south, an architectural history of Austria, for instance, might expand and contract its geographical remit along lines determined by the influence of Vienna, from duchy to Empire to Republic. Such a history of Austrian architecture would, therefore, intersect with the architectural histories of Poland and Turkey, which are themselves subject to the same problem of territorial fluidity over time. For Austria, but also Poland, Germany, the Czech Republic and other contemporary states, the added complexities introduced by migration in the eighteenth and nineteenth centuries, as well as by the mid-twentieth-century diaspora of Jewish architects, would allow some historiographical frameworks to claim buildings in the United States, South Africa and Australia as 'Austrian' (to keep to this example), or more specifically as 'Viennese', or at least bound to an Austrian or Viennese architectural patrimony.

What do the methodological divisions in architectural history of biography and geo-politics have in common? For one thing, they share the need to negotiate the balance of the general with the particular: how far can we read an individual architect's work as an index of his or her generation?

8   Whose heritage? Kaiserbad Spa (now Bath I) at Karlovy Vary, Czech Republic, architects Fellner und Helmer, Vienna 1895, atelierchef Alexander Neumann, photographer unknown.

Or the architecture of a distinct state, kingdom or region as manifestations of broader transnational or international currents? Historians of the modern movement have, in particular, faced this problem, from both biographical and geo-political perspectives. How far can architectural historians press the specificity of their subject, the irreducibility of the biographical, or of the national?

In most cases, geo-political limits offer a useful and easy way to restrict an architectural history. These limits, though, are neither natural nor static. There is much to learn of the historian's own context in the way he or she constructs a territory, geography or culture.

Type

The correlation between the form, character and organization of a building and the purpose it serves led observers in the eighteenth and nineteenth centuries to regard architecture as analogous with any number of other phenomena, natural or cultural. Like birds, paintings, rocks and people, buildings could be divided into families that could be understood independently of history. A typological approach to architectural history married the values of intellectual pragmatism with the empirical division of buildings into categories shaped by how they appeared to work. In his *Dictionnaire historique d'architecture* (1832), Antoine Quatremère de Quincy explains the nature of the term as applied to architecture:

> The word *type* presents less the image of the thing than the idea of an element which must itself serve as a rule for the model. . . . The model, understood in the sense of practical execution, is an object that should be repeated as it is; contrariwise, the *type* is an object after which each artist can conceive works that bear no resemblance to each other. All is precise and given when it comes to the model, while all is more or less vague when it comes to the *type*.[36]

As a category, then, 'type' is substantially looser than 'model', allowing for broad groupings of buildings according to shared points of reference, commonly connected to the building's purpose. Just as architecture as such can be thought to have a history, so too can its genres. Thus we can conceive of an architectural history of the hospital, the university campus, the basilica, the factory, the museum, the high-density housing block, the railway station, the opera house, the presidential library and the airport. Each family is both figural and functional in character, and further divisible according to categories that are often suggested by the type itself: ecclesiastical architecture as a type includes sub-genres shaped by liturgy, plan-form or period; likewise, convalescent hospitals, asylums for the insane, and hospitals for communicable diseases can lay claim to their own architectural histories.

Types can be intimately tied to nature, as Marc-Antoine Laugier argued in 1753: the 'primitive' hut reflected an 'ideal of perfect geometry'.[37] Trees lent columns; their boughs gave shape to a rustic pediment. In a seminal article of 1977, Anthony Vidler calls this the 'first typology'.[38] Architectural

types can also relate to their use, such as the examples introduced above, where the type can be followed historically as
a series of changes, in the first instance, to the organization
of the building plan. This is Vidler's 'second typology'. These
generic divisions tend to be extra-architectural in nature,
generated from outside of architecture and applied or evidenced in buildings. As such, these first and second typologies
run in the opposite direction to style, which, although (as we
have seen) it responds to external forces and provocations,
is basically internal to architecture.[39] Typological divisions of
one kind of ecclesiastical architectural history from another
are largely determined by religious, cultural and social factors
rather than architectural or aesthetic qualifications. Churches
that are remarkably different in appearance and that follow
distinct theories of architecture can be connected typologically on these grounds and treated as a coherent basis for
architectural history.[40]

(In addition to the categories above, Vidler also posits a
'third typology'. This concerns the autonomous, self-referen-
tial form of architectural design that gained international
currency in the 1960s and 1970s most prominently through
the architectural projects and writings of Aldo Rossi. This
third approach to building type reduces historical works of
architecture to 'architectural elements' that can be transformed into the material for design and composition. This
process very directly demonstrates the operative utility of
architectural history for architects, a theme to which we will
later return. Conceived thus, as Daniel Sherer puts it, '[T]he
type repeats nothing exactly, but reminds us, in a vague
sense . . . of earlier urban patterns and experiences.'[41])

In his introduction to *A History of Building Types* (1976),
Pevsner suggests that the need for a typological knowledge
of architectural history is connected to the widened scope of
the architect's activities in the nineteenth century. Where
architecture was once the domain of 'churches and castles
and palaces', runs Pevsner's argument, the architect is now
concerned with 'a multitude of building types'. Quoting the
American architect Henry van Brunt (in 1886), he adds to
the types named above 'churches with parlours, kitchens and
society rooms', hotels, school houses and college buildings,
skating rinks, casinos, music halls and many others that give

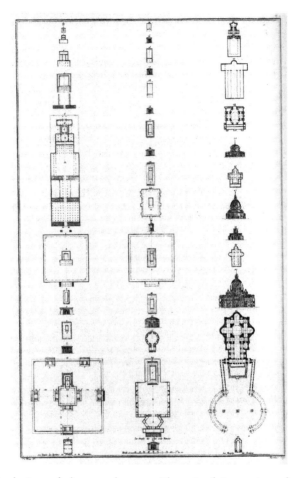

9 Evolution of the temple type, Plate 1 of *Les ruines des plus beaux monuments de la Grèce, considérées du côté de l'histoire et du côté de l'architecture*, by Julien-David Le Roy, plate by Micheli-not, after Le Moine.

us cause to consider the architect's expanded remit of the last two centuries.[42] Pevsner lists a series of architectural histories of the eighteenth and nineteenth centuries that include 'surveys of types which traditionally formed part of the architectural courses', and a number of more recent studies to complement his own attempt to provide a first history of building types written as such.[43] Carroll Meeks's *The Railroad Station* (1956) is notable among his examples, as is Johan Friedrich Geist's history of the nineteenth-century arcade, dating from 1969.[44]

Of course, Pevsner's book does not exhaust the extent of architectural types, attending mainly to those of importance to architects of the nineteenth century. In the book's foreword, though, he usefully observes that 'this treatment of buildings allows for a demonstration of development both by style and by function, style being a matter of architectural history, function of social history'.[45] Type, then, is in his presentation a combination of function, materials and styles, the histories of which intersect as a typological history informed by the demands made of architects by their clients and patrons, by the technical possibilities available to the architect, and by architecture's internal artistic and conceptual developments.[46]

Most contemporary histories of architecture that follow cues of a typological nature do not do so in order to advance a strong theory of architectural genus. For most architectural histories type is a category of convenience that combines well with other framing devices. Michael Webb's *Architecture in Britain Today* (1969) makes typological divisions in a history determined by geography and period, so that modern British architecture is further classified within a number of smaller genres: a series of educational and institutional types, houses and housing at various scales, shops and offices, sports venues and churches.[47] Typological classification is not the end for which these histories are the means, but genre offers useful divisions to an otherwise unwieldy subject.

Igea Troiani's history of the bank buildings of Australian architect Stuart McIntosh is clearly concerned with that type of work within McIntosh's œuvre.[48] She studies the evolution of his approach to the problem of designing banks, of reacting to client demands, of exploring the possibilities afforded by this kind of commission for his own thinking about architecture. These questions are thus partly biographical, partly contextual and partly periodic, relating to the history of modern architecture in general, and its Australian path in particular. Again, it would make little sense to insist on calling Troiani's approach to architectural history typological, yet in her article on McIntosh's banks she uses the tools of a typological division of architectural history, and of the architect's biography, to manage a subdivision of the larger histories to which McIntosh's case contributes.

To suggest, though, that a typological organization of individual architectural histories is often commonsensical, as in Webb's book, is not to overlook more complex historiographical manoeuvres that are likewise predicated on a typological identification.

In *Bouwen voor de Kunst?* (2006), for instance, Wouter Davidts addresses a sub-genre of the museum type, the museum of contemporary art, while conducting a critique of typological and critical categories.[49] Davidts's book reverses a simplistic typological reading while upholding the 'natural' frame suggested by his subject. He acts against the tendency of architectural histories concerned with institutions to pay too little attention to the extra-architectural forces that help to shape the building. The art gallery is for him a building and an institution, and the programme of one shapes that of the other. Davidts's study pays close attention to the workings and imperatives of art institutions while offering a historical account of the building types on which they rely.[50] This counters the tendency among architectural histories to privilege the building above the institution – reflected, of course, in those institutional histories that regard architecture and architectural decisions as incidental to the functions and ambitions of the institution being housed.

Setting aside these observations concerning overtly typologically organized architectural histories, the vast majority of histories of architecture organized along typological lines treat the functional division of one building type from another much more pragmatically, where a type is a convenient way to limit a historical study rather than constituting a fixed and defensible unit.

Technique

Earlier in this book we encountered a basic failure of architectural historians to agree on what architecture has been, historically. As we have seen, this failure has allowed for vibrant discussions and important conceptual differences that have informed a broad and rich approach to the study of architecture's past. The fact remains, though, that where some think that architectural history encompasses all building ascribed to human culture from all time, others treat it as a European tradition of mere centuries' depth.

In the last essay published before his death, Reyner Banham considered how this problem gave rise to a historiographical premise: that there is something particular to architecture of which histories can be written. Or rather: one can write histories of the things that architects do that others do not.[51] This latter distinction allows us to include proto-architects in this definition of a pretext for architectural historiography, which is to say, include those master-masons, sculptors or *proti* who would not have had the present-day concept of 'architect' available to them through historical circumstances. The question therefore becomes: what have architects done over time, which now defines them historically as architects, and their work as architecture, and of which histories can be written? Histories of this kind see coherence in the way that architects have put concepts into play over time, knowingly or not. Such histories as these might regard this as the basis of architecture's disciplinarity, rendering productive the anachronistic application of the terms 'architecture' and 'architect' to buildings that, and individuals who, were not considered as such in their own time. It links the present to the past, and allows the historian of architecture to tell a story about architecture without the burdens of that term's more recent history as a concept and an institution.

Following the lead offered by Michel Foucault, we can think of these architectural histories as histories of technique, where technique is a product of discourse. Architectural histories need not be Foucauldian in their approach or tenor to take advantage of the historical divisions that his thinking has allowed the last few decades of historiography: the history of technique *within* architecture, and of architecture *as* a technique.[52]

Consider, as examples of this broadly constituted approach, architectural histories of drawing, of tectonics, of construction, of designing for a world seen as if in pictures, of writing instructions for other architects (the Italian word *trattazione* best captures this technique), of ordering reality along architectural lines (the Italian, again, *progettazione*), or simply of making windows, doors, corners and pathways. These can equally be subject to such historicization as the long durational history of architecture allows. Giedion's *Space, Time, and Architecture* (1941) is a model of this approach to writing history: identifying in their abstraction the values and activities of the modern architect and retrospectively constructing their history.[53] His two-volume work *The Eternal Present* (1962) is likewise a classic instance of an art history of 'space-making', delving deep into Mesopotamian and Egyptian examples in order to activate a modernist teleology with a lengthy run-up.[54] Giedion's student Christian Norberg-Schulz offers a parallel example in his books *Intentions in Architecture* (1965), *Existence, Space, and Architecture* (1971) and *Meaning in Western Architecture* (1975).[55] The technique with which these are concerned is 'place-making', a phenomenological concept that acquired significant currency and historical authority through Norberg-Schulz's work. Whatever the stripe and tenor of the content of a history of technique in or as architecture, the historiographical mechanism of the *longue durée* owes a great deal to the trajectory of French historiological thought that spans from Lucien Febvre and Marc Bloch to Foucault. In the hands of Giedion and Norberg-Schulz, to give two instances drawn from many possible examples, these technical histories are less histories of architecture than of practices. These are not always, and in fact are rarely, specific to architecture. And the identification of the 'techniques' of which these historians make histories is itself a product of history. These histories would be inconceivable outside of the moment in which they were written.

More recently, John Macarthur and Antony Moulis have argued for a history of plan-making (or architectural planning) as a basis for such a long-durational history of architecture. The plan, like any other technique in architecture, is a historically shaped construction of architectural historians. For architects to think planimetrically is not a given of architecture, but rather something acquired through transmission and habit. In a paper delivered to the 2005 conference of the

Society of Architectural Historians, Australia and New Zealand (SAHANZ), Macarthur and Moulis observe one of the complications of relating the history of the architectural plan to the history of architecture: 'The plan has been an integral, general tool for architecture across diverging socio-historical circumstances, in which the concept of architecture has also varied greatly. It is difficult, then, to imagine a history of the plan that is premised on a solid concept of architecture.'[56] Even to limit the history of architecture to a Western tradition, the qualifications, skills, knowledge, tasks and status of the figure of the architect have all changed dramatically over the centuries. Beyond a loose definition of 'architecture' as 'the art or science of building', there is no unified definition of the term that has survived changes in society, technology or institutions. Macarthur and Moulis thus ask, 'what bases are there of a longitudinal history of architecture?'[57]

The plan offers an example of the kind of historical subject that might operate across other forms of historical change. It can be understood literally and conceptually. It can be found in drawings and diagrams as well as in buildings themselves. From a drawn plan the historian can extrapolate a ground plan of a building, either as a reality subject to scale or as a figure reacting to the experience of a building by its inhabitants. (The classic historical problem of this kind is to understand the building represented by Piranesi's complex, multi-level plan of the fictional Ampio Magnifico Collegio of 1750.[58]) Conversely, from an extant building the historian can diagrammatize the building at scale or in abstraction. Colin Rowe's famous historical comparisons of Renaissance and modern buildings in his essay 'The Mathematics of the Ideal Villa' are exemplary of this possibility.[59]

Historical knowledge of the plan operates between these two approaches. Planning forms a 'technique' of architecture that, while independent of the various contexts that shape any given plan (drawn or derived), can nonetheless learn from those historical contexts while overcoming the specificities of any building to understand how architecture has been sustained historically and historiographically. The plan therefore presents architectural history with the problem of whether this field of study is a branch of history or an

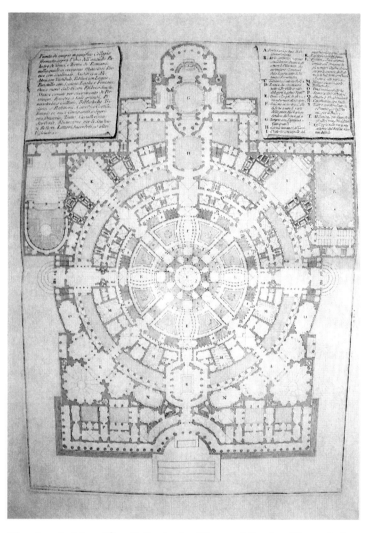

10 Ampio Magnifico Collegio, by Giovanni Battista Piranesi, first
published in his *Opera varie di architettura, prospettive, grotteschi,
antichità* (Rome: Bouchard, 1750).

expression of historical consciousness intimately tied to the work of architects.

Whatever the larger conceptual implications of this choice might be, the architectural history of planning as conceived above describes the kind of approach to historical research and working that overcomes the historical specificities of architecture's status as an art, craft, trade or profession, and thus positions continuities where other forms of history (framed by style, geography, architectural theory, society or culture) would recognize the historicity and the limitations of a general theory of architecture of which architectural historians could write histories. In this sense, the technique of planning sits alongside other techniques that have been treated historically. Each offers new filters for the subject of architecture while overcoming the limitations imposed by what we might understand as 'classic' historiographical tools and perspectives.

Theme and analogy

This sixth and final grouping of approaches to architectural historiography runs against the grain of the preceding headings. Whereas architectural history as the history of architectural style, type or technique relies on a historical continuity that can be constructed as internal to architecture, an architectural history organized along thematic or analogical lines references the relationships, concrete and abstract, between architecture and its 'exterior'. A history of architecture organized thematically concerns coincidences between architectural activity and other kinds of historical activity, between buildings and the uses to which they are put or the significance they accrue, and it also engages the realm of architectural ideas and themes, such as inhabitation and representation, which themselves have repercussions well beyond architecture. Conversely, an analogous architectural history explores the conceptual devices available to architectural historians that allow that field to contribute new perspectives on issues beyond architecture, which once seemed beyond the architectural historian's remit. How, such histories ask, is architecture analogous to technology and information systems, to politics, to society, to medicine and so on? Which of the architectural historian's tools and techniques might usefully contribute to the study of those other fields?

Architectural histories organized along these lines align with the writing genre of late-twentieth-century architectural culture usually called architectural theory. Among thematic histories we would count those that identify architecture's role in extra-architectural historical and theoretical themes, or the coincidence of architectural interests and developments with those beyond architecture. They are often recognizable by the pairing of the term 'architecture' with an external corollary: domesticity, language, the body, politics, religion, society, science, utopia, dystopia, hygiene, technology, advertising, consumption, memory, literature, film and so forth. The list is long, flexible and comprises a substantial bibliography that has dominated architectural publishing in recent decades. These histories treat the intersections and analogies to be found with and in the architectural subject. For histories conceived with these objectives in view, architecture becomes both evidence of the world of phenomena exceeding architecture itself and a player in that world.

This category might seem like a catch-all for those histories not easily associated with the preceding classifications and indeed it is the most difficult to isolate, since it opens out into a large number of disciplines beyond architecture and architectural history. Although there are indeed plentiful examples of thematic architectural histories, especially since the 1980s, they allow for an important conceptual distinction. If the *longue durée* history of architecture evidences a 'technical' or disciplinary consciousness, then thematic and analogous histories of architecture demonstrate an interdisciplinary consciousness whereby one understands where architecture sits in relation to its various physical and conceptual settings. Whereas technique concerns the core, theme and analogy pertain to the edges, and thus to the borders between architecture and other things.

An influential early example of such a thematized, theoretical architectural history is Tafuri's *Progetto e utopia* (1973), which historicized and politicized the interaction of architecture and ideology after the Enlightenment.[60] In addition to Tafuri's own books on political and ideological themes, which concern settings as diverse as Vienna, the Soviet Union, Venice, Rome, the United States and Germany, a steady stream of publications have followed his cues or established new entries to this subject.[61] It is reasonable that politics would present an early locus for thematic histories of architecture. A thematic approach, as it was first tested, had a political mission in relation to the traditional techniques for researching, organizing and writing architectural history.[62] Organization along thematic lines permitted historians to account for evidence and analytical perspectives for which a history of style, for instance, or type simply did not allow. The historical studies presented in the American journal *Oppositions* (1973–84) explored many of the implications of this historiographical theme (alongside, notably, the theme of language). In its uptake of the *Oppositions* project, the later journal *Assemblage* (1986–2000) advanced this theme through its preoccupation with representation.

William J. Mitchell's *City of Bits* (1995) might now seem naïve as a study in the architectural parallels offered by the 'Netscape' generation of internet life ('Now, I just said that wjm@mit.edu was my name, but you might equally well [or equally inappositely] claim that it was my address'[63]). His book was, nonetheless, one of the first to open architectural theory to this theme, and to explore problems of the newly broadened experiences of networked life. It also offers a useful example of a strategic dislocation of architectural themes and theories from architecture *qua* architecture. Mitchell trades physical space for virtual space, studying the manner in which online communities were built and maintained in parallel to communities contingent on the occupation of land and three-dimensional space. Within a theoretical-critical approach he seeks to understand the nature of the infrastructure necessary to conduct business, communicate and otherwise interact virtually, all the aspects of a way of life that quickly became the norm. Positioned thus, architecture and its theory had a new role in bridging existing and emerging phenomena critically, theoretically and historically. Mitchell's *City of Bits* might now be a historical record of this turn in its own right, sitting alongside Jean-François Lyotard's *Moralités postmodernes* (1993) or

Douglas Coupland's *Microserfs* (1995) as evidence of a mid-1990s fascination with this techno-cultural theme.[64] Importantly, though, Mitchell demonstrated the conceptual and historical availability of architecture and its lessons for problems beyond architecture.

Other examples illustrate how architecture and the tools of its historians offer new takes on existing themes. Dietrich Neumann's book *Film Architecture* (1999) explores the cross-pollination of the two terms of his title over the lifespan of modern film. Steven Jacobs pushes this theme further in his study *The Wrong House: The Architecture of Alfred Hitchcock* (2007), where modern architecture and the Hitchcock filmography together consider the themes of psychology and space along historical and critical lines, and within the history of techniques of cinematic production.

A number of anthologies have, similarly explored questions of gender in architectural history: *Sexuality and Space*, *The Sex of Architecture* and *Stud*, to name some 1990s classics.[65]

11   Jeffries apartment and courtyard, West 10th St, Greenwich Village, New York, depicted in *Rear Window*, directed by Alfred Hitchcock (1954). Production photograph.

None of these books' editors or authors would unconditionally position these as volumes of architectural history, especially given their shared mission to open up knowledge of the canon with the tools developed by post-structuralist and postcolonial theory imported into the historiography of architecture and theorization of historical architectural works and themes. As a result, these works and themes definitively extend their historical subjects by the use of new critical and theoretical perspectives, all the while cutting through the chronological divisions established and maintained in the nineteenth and twentieth centuries. Architectural histories that take their subjects as participants in a broader, extra-architectural theme, or that offer analogies with other historical phenomena, can extend the canon by reinstalling figures and works overlooked and then forgotten by previous critics and historians of architecture. They often do this by addressing an existing canon with new analytical tools that render an established historical subject even more complex, thereby valorizing its importance while questioning the mechanisms of the canon itself.

Doubtless there are further approaches to the problem of organizing the past of architecture into historical units to which I could devote space here. Some of the choices available to contemporary historians of architecture have endurance on their side; others are relatively new, bound to the increasingly relativist and contextualist tendencies of all kinds of historiography during the latter part of the twentieth century. As strong strategies, they are all subject to intellectual fashion. As softer frameworks or approaches to the writing of architectural history, tempered one by another, or by others, they describe a good number of the organizational devices used by historians to convert the vast, heterogeneous past of architecture into coherent histories. Where this chapter has considered the terms on which historians can enact this translation, the next will turn to the stuff of that past. What of the past survives to the present as the material of architectural history? We are speaking now of the *content* of architectural history, and inevitably, therefore, of its relation to *evidence*.

3
Evidence

It seems straightforward to observe that the content of architectural history is architecture, historically considered. We can expand this observation, though, to say that architectural history is also the history of architecture's relations with artefacts, settings and historical problems that are neither architecture, as it might be defined in any given moment, nor architectural in nature. But what, then, *is* architecture for it to have a history? Or an 'outside'? These questions suppose a conceptual coherence to the term 'architecture' over a period of time, which is not at all a given. We could therefore rephrase to ask, what *has* architecture been, insofar as its definition is, for us, something of a moving target? How is architecture made, or how *has* it been made or, post-factum, defined and appropriated? Why does the category or term 'architecture' suit some kinds of creative, cultural and technical activity better than others that likewise result in buildings – or in cities, landscapes or works of art? These are clearly theoretical questions as much as they are historical and they concern the disciplinary knowledge of architecture as well as its history. To the extent that these questions can be found in architecture and asked of its past, however, their answers rely on the bodies of evidence available to historians of architecture and the conceptual premises that limit the extent of that evidence. We have considered some aspects of the latter in the previous chapter; now we turn to the way that evidence interacts with conceptual parameters. Architectural historians pose their questions of evidence, but the questions that are available to historians depend on theories of architectural history, to which historians knowingly or subconsciously subscribe, that restrict the scope or import of the evidence itself. Given these contingencies, the pool of evidence for an architectural historian might include buildings, spaces, ruins, cities and infrastructure; it might also include procedural and design documents, commissioning notes and contract documents, schedules of quantities and correspondence with clients and authorities; it might include any manner or representations of the 'finished' work, from watercolours and engravings to depictions on television and in advertising; it can include oral histories, letters between colleagues or friends or relatives, newspaper reviews, and ephemeral residues of all kinds, from tangible documents to the realm of ideas.

It is safe to say that today there are few if any limits placed upon the forms of evidence employed by historians of architecture, from the building that resists time to the evanescent trace that is at time's perpetual mercy. This has not, however, always been the case. The relatively wide acceptance of an open field of evidence has been a hard-won battle of the twentieth century's later decades. It has much to do with shifts over this same period of time in the appreciation of what architecture itself can be. Indeed, whether the subject of architectural history is a building, a historiographical theme or a biographical figure, it is defined against a concept of architecture and the architect. Historical research then opens these concepts up to scrutiny. Given the iterative character of this perpetual exchange between research, knowledge and concepts, there is no stability to the concept of architecture, past or present. An architectural history can tell its readers what *is* known and *can be* known of the past. These are questions of evidence.

Few thesis advisers would suggest that a Ph.D. student in architectural history research an architect with few extant buildings, no known archive or body of 'paper' architecture, and little presence in the architectural magazines of his or her day. Such a project might bear an unpredictably high yield of fruit, but it would be a risky investment – think of the poor fortunes of Phineas G. Nanson in A. S. Byatt's *The Biographer's Tale*.[1] This is not to suggest that historians of architecture have failed to take such gambles. For some this merely makes the research more challenging – and more rewarding. Architectural historians have in recent decades borrowed and developed a number of tools to neutralize the effect of the apparent absence of traditional forms of evidence for emerging problems in architectural history and historiography. Especially has this been so in the postcolonial historiography of architecture and in sexuality- and gender-based revisionist histories, which confront and undermine the monolithic, hetero-masculine and Western perspectives and categories that shaped the modern field for its first century, and which persist today.[2] Yet from the most traditional to the most experimental approaches to the writing of architectural history, the basic point stands: an architectural historian will have either knowledge or intuition about the material on which they might base their study, and where it might be found. The scale of available evidence will inform the scale of the work attempted by the historian.

To recap: architecture is architectural history's substance. The material, ephemeral and conceptual traces of that content are architectural history's evidence. The definition of architecture as a subject of historical study lies between architectural history's conceptual and technical content and its traces in the world. This definition of architecture's historical extent can be made as broad or as narrow as the architectural historian can justify on conceptual, epistemological or evidentiary grounds. An evidentiary field reflecting the historian's view will, however, serve his or her construal of the historical (and by extension contemporary) architectural subject.

Where issues of approach – method, frame, conceptual presuppositions – determine the shape of an architectural history, the concomitant limitations placed by the architectural historian upon their material will inform the matter of that history, and ultimately the kinds of conclusions available to the historian. A history concerning the recovery of a design decision does not necessarily need to have recourse to the same kind of evidence as a history concerning the social significance of a particular public or semi-public site. These are different kinds of questions, and their 'answers' rely upon different kinds of material – and by extension upon different analytical tools. The form and content of architectural history, its method and evidence, thus assume a dialectical relationship. One tests the other and vice versa. The extent to which a document is useful depends on the questions asked of it. And the pertinence of the question will be judged by what is known or knowable of the subject to hand.

The juridical allusion is apt, because the idea of 'evidence' invokes the courtroom setting and the question of 'proof'. It concerns analytical weight and judgement; cause, measurable effect and plausibility. The architectural historian sometimes acts as an advocate, presenting the available evidence in order to represent and reconstruct, on the basis of 'proof', past events, decisions, procedures and relationships. He or she employs the rhetorical arts and narrative structures. As a judge, the architectural historian then weighs the balance of what we might reasonably deduce from the material and circumstances of any given historical case or problem. The insistence of the historian's conclusions will depend on the strength and weight of the evidence he or she can advance as a defensible case. All of this happens within any given history of architecture, and the historian plays both these roles, of advocate and judge, out of necessity. History can only ever represent the past, though, and only a foolhardy historian would position their conclusions as definitive for time immemorial. New evidence comes to light, new conceptual perspectives and analytical tools alter the significance of existing evidence. While these issues are hardly particular to architectural history, in reading and writing the history of architecture we can find a number of evidentiary issues to which architecture, as a subject of historical study, lends specific form.

Evidence and architectural history

When the subject of an architectural history is a building or monumental sculpture, we can learn how it was commissioned, designed and realized. We can rely on various forms of evidence to understand how the design changed over the course of the project, from conception to completion, and suggest reasons for those changes. We can propose the meaning a subject of historical study once projected or accrued, and how that might have changed or remained consistent over time. Depending on the qualifications we use, we can ask the evidence to help us to decide whether or not any particular work forms part of the history of architecture. Is it canonical? Or peripheral? Taking another angle, do certain kinds of evidence pose problems for the historian's approach, tools, analysis, argument or conclusions? For all of these questions, evidence maintains a crucial role in mediating the relationship between historical problems and their analysis. The way that evidence is understood by the architectural historian doubtless informs the way that his or her work is conceived, researched, documented and presented. 'Work' here means both the subject of study and the medium of the architectural history. As discussion around the recently launched multi-media edition of the *JSAH* recognizes, some forms of evidence and modes of analysis demand a different approach to publication from that which books and other traditional print-media can sustain.[3] Any position, implicit or explicit, on an item of historical evidence will shape how research is resolved as history and therefore will inform the process by which a fragmented and disarticulated knowledge of the past becomes historical narrative.

Just knowing that something happened is rarely significant in its own terms, or perhaps goes only so far as to fill out a little more of the infinite breadth and depth of what Fernand Braudel called 'total' history.[4] In architecture, the survival from a distant past of a building, monument or the configuration of an urban zone is proof enough of that artefact's having been made, from which we can draw certain assumptions, the facts of which we might be able to recover and test: somebody commissioned and paid for it, somebody coordinated its construction, somebody took decisions on how it would look and from what it would be made, somebody inhabited it or the space around it. The extent to which we can deduce the particulars of a building's past from the building itself is limited by the kinds of documents and traces that point to answers to those issues, as well as by their reliability, which will be subject to any number of measures.

Put simply, what is properly evidential at any given moment or for any given problem in the history of architecture is ultimately a conceptual issue, with positions by no means fixed and by no means the subject of any consensus. Certain materials will shed light on the questions of 'what', 'how', 'where', 'who' and 'when', but 'why' will always require more deduction than these and demand different analytical tools. Admittedly, these observations are most easily addressed to an overly strict view on architectural history as a history of buildings and the built environment, and invoke a basic set of materials that a historian of architecture might consult in his or her research.

Consider how issues concerning evidence relate to two of architectural historiography's traditional problems: the history of the building, and the history of the architect (and of his or her buildings as an œuvre). As we briefly noted above, the close study of the building might take in its representation in painting, etching, bas-relief, photography, journalistic or professional criticism, popular imagery or literature; the design drawings, tender notices, working drawings, circulation studies, sketches of on-site modifications to the architectural scheme, preparatory studies, building logbooks, graffiti; correspondence between the architect and his or her client, between the client and his or her financiers, between the architect and the project's specialists, colleagues, friends and family, or between any combination of architect, client and municipal, regional or state authority. Such evidence, taken together, might tell the historian a great deal about the building and the circumstances of its design, construction and life as a finished work.

To understand a building's place in the œuvre of the architect, for instance, one would need to take into account the trajectory and content of that œuvre, the range of influences (strong and weak) working thereupon – from the seemingly obvious to the indirect and happenstantial – the sources used and references made by the architect, and the architect's ambitions for his or her practice, be they intellectual, aesthetic, social or technical, and whether they be recorded or open to deduction. Here surveys of magazines, studies of telephone books and business directories, calls for tender, epistolary archives and oral histories can become important

12 Poster advertising the Exhibition of Seventy Drawings by Francesco Borromini from the Albertina of Vienna at the Gabinetto Nazionale delle Stampe, Rome, 1958–9.

tools for placing the architect in his or her intellectual and professional context and for ordering the chronology of his or her practice. Much of this material is the stuff of all manner of histories, and architectural history borrows extensively from those historiographical strategies that privilege evidence that might otherwise be considered incidental and minor.

As limited as these two examples and the questions they pose may be, they have extended applications in studies concerning architecture as a setting for social and cultural behaviour, trade and exchange, political and religious events, or as a knowledge system, or an analogy or interlocutor for parallel historical problems. Such extensions as these furthermore revisit the place of certain forms of evidence and their status for the architectural historian's traditional questions and problems, thereby forcing these questions and the materials to which they were addressed to adapt to and accommodate new perspectives and agendas within architectural historiography.

A broader, more generous and more contemporary definition of architectural history's scope would include a correspondingly wider definition of evidence. Architectural histories of recent decades draw from a range of media and sources and take an open view of the status of both. This shift away from a more constrained view of 'proper' evidence has learned from a number of broader historiographical developments of the twentieth century, which (especially from the end of the 1960s) aided the broad reformulation of architecture as a practice, culture and discourse. An architectural history might now, for example, take architecture's representation in photography as its subject. A collection of colour slides or touristic postcards could pose its own questions within the disciplinary ambit of architectural history. They would not necessarily comprise evidence towards another kind of history more overtly concerned with buildings, although they could do this too. Contemporary historical research into the cultural, sociological and intellectual dimensions of architectural culture no longer take the study of architecture as such (buildings, city centres, monuments) as their sole end.

These observations are not meant to suggest that the traditional tasks of a modern, academic architectural history are complete. Nor do they imply that the kinds of evidence to which historians of architecture have turned throughout the last century no longer serve any function for contemporary architectural historiography. Questions about the conception and construction of buildings, and about the people who design them, continue to dominate the field, even if they have made room for other means of approaching architecture historically. Historians once asked their questions of the canon's artful buildings alone. Over the course of the twentieth century the field opened up to include drawings and such other documents as Burckhardt described as appropriate for the (nineteenth-century) study of culture. This evidences an increasingly generous approach to the rapport between historical problems concerning architecture and their attendant fields of evidence.

Categories of evidence

As an account of the past of architecture, architectural history inevitably advances or reinforces a historical definition of architecture along with the historical preconditions of the term's contemporary limitations. What does present-day knowledge of architecture allow us to call 'architecture' historically? And what did people of the past call (what we now call) architecture? In this light, the material narrated by architectural histories serves as a form of authority against which can be measured the answer to the first of these questions. The means by which that material is narrated tracks a form of enquiry into the second. The questions 'What is architecture?' and 'What was architecture?' therefore serve the architectural historian to different ends. Since the historian asks these questions through the analysis and appraisal of his or her materials, the same may be said of these, too. The relation of history to evidence, for instance, is one specifically concerning 'how' and 'when' a building came to be, along with the attendant issues of 'what' (the nature of the artefact and its significance), 'why' (the reasons for this nature, the intentions of the author, the preconditions governing appearance and technical issues) and 'who' (concerning the artefact's origins both as an authored work and as a work realized under specific social, cultural, political, economic or religious conditions). With some limitations, such questions as these serve as well in their abstraction for prefabricated housing in Sub-Saharan Africa as for English stately homes. But the 'what' of architectural history turns quickly to architecture's definition in terms of traditions, aesthetic criteria and theoretical content. Debates around the issue notwithstanding, what could be called architecture by critical consensus in 1920 had changed substantially by 1960 and dramatically by the end of the twentieth century. As a result, architectural historians might now begin with a building as easily as they might end with one or evade building altogether. 'How' or 'when' might now be asked of a document or subject that would have been inconceivable as an architectural historian's subject in 1960, 1970 or even 1980.

Given these observations, we might think of the way that historical evidence bears upon conceptual questions and issues of significance according to three fluid and overlapping categories of evidence: procedural, contextual and conceptual. *Procedural evidence* leads us to the facts of any given subject: how things came to be from start to finish, and who was involved at each step of the way. The question of personnel pertains also to *contextual evidence*, which places the historical subject in its broader settings. Proof of timing, sequence, location, as well as of the figures involved and their relation to other figures – when, where and who – helps historians to place their subject in relation to other subjects and, ultimately, to the wider web of narrative accounts of the historical past against which all historians of architecture measure their work and have it assessed by others. A third category, *conceptual evidence*, concerns the kind of material that forces the question of a subject's qualification. It will often be impossible or undesirable to place a document, building or print into one categorical box or another. The disciplinary qualifications of an architectural history demand, however, a position (even implicit) on how a non-canonical or marginal subject has significance for the wider discipline – and therefore a place in what has variously been called the discourse or conversation of architectural history. The deployment of evidence in pursuit of historiographical questions or historical acuity consequently raises conceptual issues alongside those of procedure and context.

Evidence and the architectural historian's practice

A series of examples allows us to see how these points may operate in practice. Specialists in the history of architectural artefacts, design-and-construction documents, and representations of architecture, be they anticipatory, documentary or critical, have over decades adapted extensively from a range of historical and other analytical practices in order to penetrate deeper and deeper into existing historical problems. Techniques and technologies proper to surveying, engineering and other fields that demand precise measurement of all manner of dimensions, for instance, have been adapted to make exact surveys of buildings and archaeological sites – exactitude being, of course, relative. Centuries-old problems like the dimensions of columns relative to the theory of columnar heights and diameters remain, consequently, open to debate.

In this vein, a recent article by Matthew A. Cohen in the *JSAH* documents a new survey of the old Sacristy of the Basilica of San Lorenzo (Florence, 1420–9), commonly regarded as Filippo Brunelleschi's canonical contribution to the foundation of the Florentine architectural Renaissance.[5] Cohen conducts a 'rigorous observation' of the building, making a fresh study of its elements and general proportional system. He presents measured drawings and graphic analysis alongside a historical argument concerning the building's authorship, which is based on his empirical findings. He concludes that responsibility for part of the design of San Lorenzo lies with Brunelleschi's predecessor, Prior Matteo di Bartolommeo Dolfini. Cohen's analysis suggests that, as much as San Lorenzo might be understood as a building heralding new beginnings, it ought also to be understood in terms of the fourteenth-century compositional and construction practices that endured into the fifteenth century, and therefore in terms of a medieval tradition that casts a long shadow over the Renaissance. If this building can be understood, in part, as medieval, where does that leave the category and chronology of the Renaissance? In his conclusion Cohen goes only as far as recognizing that such questions are at stake in his 'critical study of architectural proportion as historical evidence'. He observes: 'This integrated, observation-based approach to the study of architectural history has the potential to bring to light new knowledge pertaining not only to architectural proportion, but to many other areas of architectural theory and practice as well.'[6]

The measurement of columnar spacing and dimensions does not, in itself, lead to a 'natural' classification of a building as either late medieval or early Renaissance. Before the middle of the nineteenth century, buildings of the fifteenth century were not considered Renaissance because the category had yet to be introduced into the tools of (then) cultural history. Cohen's study offers the valuable reminder that the 'old' task of understanding the past through the empirical study of artefacts has hardly been exhausted by work done to date. Historians can interpret new data and recalculate proportional relationships in light of other kinds of knowledge of the building, its procurement, design and fabrication. Such studies as these force us continually to reconsider the broad classifications of architectural history. As an example speaking to the forms of evidence considered in the previous section, this case treats new measurements of the building as procedural evidence, which is considered in light of contextual factors and is presented in full awareness of its conceptual implications.

Cohen's article raises the problem of how a fine-grained re-appraisal of existing evidence (through re-measurement, in his case) throws light upon a category that has implications for the historiography of an entire epoch. Our next example concerns a specialist problem in the œuvre of Piranesi: how and in what order did he compose his *Vedute di Roma* (pub-

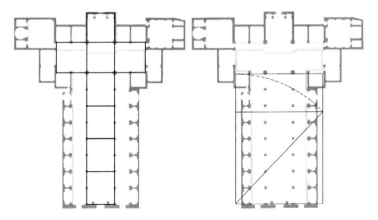

13 Measured drawing and geometrical study of San Lorenzo, Florence, by Matthew A. Cohen. By permission of Matthew A. Cohen.

lished from 1748), and when and how did he revise them over time? In her contribution to *The Serpent and the Stylus*, Roberta Battaglia demonstrates that these questions demand of historians that they understand Piranesi's procedure and its material traces in the copperplates on which he worked and in the prints made from these plates.[7] Her example is typical of the common problem of chronology posed by discovery of a new exemplar of a series, which must be dated and reconciled with the existing sequence of engravings on the basis of a specialist knowledge of the architect's works and design method.

Piranesi almost never dated his *Vedute*. He reworked the copperplates of this and other series, leaving scholars to determine the original sequence of the initial etchings and the order in which details were added, enhanced and lost through a series of revisions to the plate. Study of this problem proceeds by a comparative study of the various states of the etchings, through analysis of the deterioration and obfuscation of details on the extant copperplates, by observing the relative density of the ink on the page in any given example, along with the clarity of the print's lines, and by accounting for known patterns of sale and dispersal and the collection history of known early examples. In her essay Battaglia describes a hitherto unknown collection of the *Vedute* found in a volume of miscellaneous prints housed at the Biblioteca Apostolica Vaticana in Rome. She records in detail the fourteen *Vedute* found in this volume, comparing the examples to hand with existing known and dated collections: 'The Vatican series is of extreme interest because it contains – for some of the views – a first state not hitherto recorded in specialist studies. It also enables us to witness closely Piranesi's creative process, fixing a precise moment of that continuous and almost exasperated experimentation that the artist applied in his every working process.'[8] The evidence sheds light on a narrow problem of chronology, while opening its procedural implications to the larger question of how Piranesi designed, and thus of how he saw the world and the possibilities open to him as an architect – a question as pertinent to the *Vedute* as to his other series and to his vast work of preparing, publishing, reproducing and distributing his prints, of which thousands of examples exist worldwide.

Brunelleschi and Piranesi: these are doubtless figures of the contemporary canon of architectural history, as much as we can speak of a present-day canon. As such, the evidentiary and procedural problems they pose are somewhat traditional. The historians cited above measure and compare artefacts and determine chronologies and provenance. A third case allows us to pursue such problems as these, but by introducing the kind of esoteric materials that resist, as we will see, the firm questions and strong conclusions towards which the previous examples tend.

Moving now to a twentieth-century subject, equally canonical, a paper by Antony Moulis shows how an archival curiosity found in the Fondation Le Corbusier (Paris) muddies existing, and plausible, explanations of the origins of his plan for the Punjab capital of Chandigarh.[9] Moulis writes of a chance meeting in Bogotá, Colombia, between Le Corbusier and an Australian agronomist named Hugh C. Trumble, in which the latter described the basic layout and salient features of his home town, Adelaide, the colonial capital of South Australia designed by Colonel William Light in 1836. Under Trumble's guidance, it seems, Le Corbusier made a drawing of the city (dated 19 September 1950).

The facts proven by this drawing are relatively banal, locating both men in a certain place at a certain time, but Moulis argues its historical significance on two grounds. The first is conceptual. Le Corbusier's drawing of Adelaide shows how he understood and idealized an unsighted historical city with eyes conditioned by universalizing modernist planning concerns: 'The "Adelaide" produced by Le Corbusier (one that he pictures back to himself in drawing) is an efficacious representation of the architect's ideology on urbanism – appearing like a self-fulfilling prophecy of CIAM [the Congrès International d'Architecture Moderne] ideals in sketch form. Indeed it is through the process of "re-drawing" Adelaide that this ideology achieves what seems a perfect clarity.'[10] Its second significance is procedural and contextual. The Adelaide plan was made only days before Le Corbusier was commissioned to design the masterplan of Chandigarh and seven months before that design was resolved. Comparison of the two cities demonstrates that Le Corbusier's Adelaide and Chandigarh have much in common. As diagrams, they

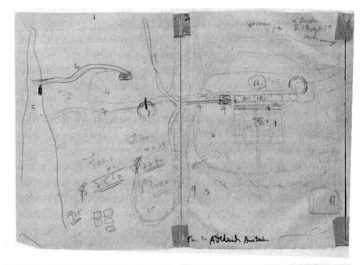

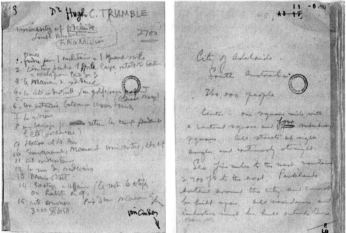

14   Adelaide, South Australia, drawn by Le Corbusier with Hugh
Trumble, Bogotá, Colombia, 1950.

share such features as plan form, disposition of elements,
location of parks and green space, relationship to landscape
forms and so forth.[11] They are both documents of a kind:
one a drawing that transcribes an existing city; the other a
city-as-document, an entirely new capital city containing

traces of its conception and implementation and all the competing forces necessarily in play.

To what, Moulis asks, does this evidence add up? He argues that, despite whatever interest Le Corbusier's Adelaide drawing might have as a curiosity and despite the context of its production with Trumble in Bogotá, the Adelaide drawing cannot be brought solidly to bear upon the analysis and interpretation of Chandigarh's design. Nevertheless, given the similarity of the two documents and the proximity of their production it legitimately works as a foil to the common suite of references that explain the Punjab city's origins.

In each of these instances evidence works conditionally to undermine a given knowledge of the subject: the authorship of San Lorenzo, the order of states in Piranesi's *Vedute*, and the origins of Le Corbusier's Chandigarh. Cohen, Battaglia and Moulis each resist unequivocal claims for the significance of their material other than to put new evidence into play with old problems. Their combined effect – to which we can add all other such efforts in the present-day field of architectural history – is to advance new knowledge while destabilizing the parameters of historical knowledge. As such, each in their own way, they illustrate the claims famously made in Carlo Ginzburg's 1979 essay 'Spie' – a classic reading on the nature and deployment of historical evidence.[12]

The medical diagnostician has to reconcile the general and typical presentations of a condition with its idiosyncratic presentation in a specific patient. Historical problems in architecture, as for any field of historiography, inevitably fail to manifest the same forms of evidence from case to case. The evidentiary field that attends to one historical problem, therefore, is bound to differ in its utility or significance from the evidence that accumulates around another. This situation calls for the historian to develop a diagnostician's instinct based on accumulated knowledge and intuition acquired over time. Experience will inform the historian's approach to the inevitable negotiation between the particularities of a case and its common characteristics. The architectural historian has a sense of how things might have been in the setting of his or her particular historical problem and draws on that knowledge and experience to get from one secure footing to the next and to propose (within reason, and limits) what might have occurred in between. These intermediate phases between one moment of relative analytical security and the next are the rightful domain of interpretation. As Ginzburg later observes in his 1991 polemical judicial history *Il giudice e lo storico*, 'A historian has the right to detect a problem where a judge might find an "absence of grounds for proceedings".'[13]

Architecture as historical evidence

These three brief examples attend to the way that evidence operates within some of the more central problems of architectural history: processes and circumstances of design, dating and attribution of works, influences and references invoked by the architect, and so forth. It is possible for architectural historians to treat the world of architecture hermetically, as presenting a set of self-contained problems and motivations. Architecture, of course, is also present in a world that pays little heed to its internal concerns. In this light, architectural works of all kinds can themselves become evidence for historical problems that are not architectural, posed by intellectual history, social history, population history, cultural history, institutional history, military history, history of religion, history of science, political history, national and area histories and so forth, not to mention art history, the history of technology and construction, or urban history – all of which come close to the way that the history of architecture attends to architectural subjects.

Consider how anthropomorphism and the divinity of the measurements derived from the ideal human body (made in God's image) diminished in Italian architecture of the sixteenth and seventeenth centuries following its instigation in the fifteenth century as part of a Christianized re-appraisal of antiquity. As much as the problems facing architects (then) and thus architectural historians (today) are particular to the fields of architecture and art, the architectural works of this era nonetheless shed light on the intellectual processes of the religious, cultural and political crises experienced by the once-totalizing Christian church in view of the Reformation.

Consider, too, how documentation of the organization, disposition and construction of the town of Thérouanne, in the Pas-de-Calais of the French northwest, might help historians to understand the military strategies, techniques and technologies of Charles V, whose army razed it to the ground in 1553 and erased its existence by laying salt on the agricultural land to prevent any possibility of its renewal. These events are not obviously the architectural historian's domain, but knowledge of the town and city, the organization of the siege and its attendant fortifications, as well as the process of the town's dismantling and destruction can enrich the historical subject proper and open architectural history to new perspectives.[14]

The historian of culture or of technology might likewise consider the nineteenth-century buildings of New Zealand Maori as indices of certain attitudes towards cultural and technological transmission and adaptation in the wake of British colonization and settlement (from 1840). Such a history might concern the nineteenth-century and twentieth-century development of building forms and arrangements, the development of fortification techniques, the adaptation of British and European architectural precedents for Maori building, and such building technologies as paint and nails. These historical developments have, in turn, implications for the social, cultural, religious and artistic histories of Maori.[15]

Along with all those other works of various media that we might call architecture, buildings are shaped by legislation, technology, taste, convention and use. They therefore allow insight into the broader historical conditions in which they were made and inhabited, and therefore become useful documents for any number of cognate historical specializations. But architecture's appearance among the field of evidence gathered around a particular historiographical problem is no guarantee of its direct availability to a historian. Especially for those architectural historians trained first as architects, a privileged insight into the process from design to realization to occupation would allow the historian of architecture to assess where architectural works, as evidence, bear upon issues that would be the proper domain of another kind of historical specialist, in a world where the line between one kind of history and another were clearer. The questions asked of a building by an economic historian, for instance, may differ markedly from the architectural historian's questions. There remains, here, an open issue of specialization and its limits: what determines whether a history is architectural? As Andrew Ballantyne has observed, 'Buildings, especially when they are aggregated into cities, are the largest artefacts.' Consequently, they are important and interesting to many others apart from architects and architectural historians. For the latter, though, he raises a fundamental issue: 'What values inform our judgement when we decide what it is that is most important to write about? And what is it that we choose to say about the buildings we decide to include in our histories?'[16]

One final example allows us pursue this idea further. The 2007 exhibition 'Twilight of the Plan' (Accademia di Architettura, Mendrisio), curated by architect and planner Josep Acebillo and architectural historians Maristella Casciato and Stanislaus von Moos, treats the two contemporaneously planned cities of Chandigarh (Le Corbusier, Pierre Jeanneret and others, from 1951) and Brasília (Lucio Costa and Oscar Niemeyer, 1956–60) as a form of historical *material*.[17] In his catalogue essay 'Vers une "Grille ChaBra"', von Moos describes the exhibition's conceptual and curatorial challenges. His comments bear strongly upon the problem of balancing between the 'interior' and 'exterior' of a historical architectural subject:

> The pictures shown in the exhibition document the paradigms for which those cities have either been admired or criticized: the triumphalism of their governmental palaces, though 'broken' in the case of Chandigarh, the vast open ('oceanic') spaces around them, the rhetoric of progress as dramatized in their traffic arteries (an infrastructure that has generated higher traffic densities in both cities than anywhere else in their respective countries), and the confidence in the welfare state as reflected in their carefully designed, yet stereotyped housing schemes. Also shown, of course, are the gaps that exist between the projects as they were planned and built on the one hand and the way they have been occupied, used, or re-defined during the past decades on the other, and the breaks and fissures through which the realities of poverty and

the promises of globalization invade the once relatively 'cartesian' spaces.[18]

Engaging with these historiographical problems, *Twilight of the Plan* presented archival photographs documenting the early life of the two planned cities, but turns quickly to the present moment as surveyed (2006) by photographer Enrico Cano. Thus it speaks not only to the process of conception and realization but also to the history of the city as a setting for modern life. The images might offend a puritan modernist, but they describe a reality that *includes* architecture while refusing the kinds of limits that architecture (and architectural history) might impose, in order to understand the way that these cities and their buildings operate as a setting for all manner of social, familial and cultural activities.

Interior and exterior histories

When a work of architecture is itself evidence for a non-architectural problem in history, as a document it internalizes the evidentiary field that would otherwise have been important for analysis of the building as a subject of architectural history. The building, drawing, photograph or urban block thus indexes an internally complex field of forces and decisions. An example of a mass housing project might, for example, be read as a simple artefact in a history, say, of housing economics, or as a given consequence within the mechanisms of housing policy and production. An architectural historian might be inclined to dig deeper into the project itself to understand how its production and appearance attend to its role and function in housing. Someone, after all, took the policy and effected the translation that made the architecture look a certain way; someone (else) defined how an individual building within the project might relate to another; someone (perhaps different again) determined how the housing scheme would be promoted to would-be inhabitants. For each of these problems, the historian of architecture has recourse to evidence that straddles a division between specialized and non-specialized.

As much as a building can be understood to inform historical issues that are well beyond the field of architecture, drawing the architectural historian's perspective into these historical issues can render buildings a richer source without reconstituting the problems as architectural in nature. Writing of the specific historiographical problems presented by medieval architecture and the medieval architect, Nicole Coldstream observes: 'Once a building is completed it may continue to have a personal history. But it will also enter the main historical narrative, a narrative that encompasses far more than understanding how a building is made.'[19] The degree to which an 'architectural' knowledge of the building is important to understanding how it enters the 'main historical narrative' determines the extent to which the specialized approach to historical evidence exercised by historians of architecture will be important for unpacking the historical question posed by or of the example at hand.

4
How useful?

The past has long offered the architect a series of models, provocations and inspirations, which have to a varying extent helped to shape his or her artistic and professional practice. The introduction of Roman antiquity as a source of formal and typological models in fifteenth-century Florence and Rome witnesses the emergence of a new awareness of the past and its importance for the present. We can now call this new conceptual relationship an emergent historical consciousness. As such, this sense of historicity makes up part of the foundations of modern architectural culture; even when an architectural movement, like the Bauhaus, has taken a rhetorical stance against historical models and precedents, it has been aware of the historicity of its choices.[1] Architects not only quote from the past, they also assess their work and the concept of contemporary architecture against historical measures. For several centuries architecture maintained this relationship with antiquity, but it extends well beyond this particular point of reference. Focillon, for example, explains the cyclical recurrence of historical forms in *La vie des formes* (1934); Colin Rowe explores the relationship of modernism to the Renaissance on 'rational' grounds in 'The Mathematics of the Ideal Villa' (1947); Zevi insists on the importance of a mannerist archetype for the post-war modernist in *Michelangiolo architetto* (1964); and Tafuri argues the dangers of architectural historians seeing too many lessons in the past in his book *Teorie e storia dell'architettura* (1968).[2]

From the eighteenth century onwards it became clear that one could study architectural history as a dimension of the study of human culture, for its own sake, as well as for the lessons it might offer architects working in the present moment. Architects engaged historical knowledge of architecture as a traditional knowledge open to contestation and development, and as a lexicon of examples that could be invoked almost as curios. Many writers have drawn the parallel between the illustrated histories of architecture that began to appear in the middle decades of the nineteenth century, such as Quatremère de Quincy's *Dictionnaire historique d'architecture* (1832) or Joseph Gwilt's *An Encyclopædia of Architecture* (1842), and the 'encyclopedic' displays enacted in the picturesque and folly gardens like Retz near Paris, the Swedish King Gustavus III's gardens at Haga and Drottningholm, or the Russian landscapes described in Andreas Schönle's *The Ruler in the Garden* (2007).[3] The great eclectic debates of the mid to late nineteenth century relied on the availability of architectural history to those who were designing buildings.[4] The significance and propriety of styles and decorations were treated as codified and fixed by some and regarded as arbitrary by others. They were, nonetheless, available to the architect like patterns in a book of samples, retaining meaning at some level but no longer contingent on the place and time in which they first appeared.

These examples serve to demonstrate the tendency, fully exercised in the twentieth century, to divorce the usefulness of architectural history for the designing architect from the precise circumstances of that history as it might be understood by a historian. It is hard to ignore the tendency of architects to find in history something useful, be it models, concepts, strategies, provocations or inspiration. This sense of architectural history's import lends a qualification for the works of architecture's historical canon and the terms and means of its revision over time. It has also shaped how architectural history is taught in schools of architecture and has thus informed the structure of the problem of historical instrumentalization for architecture well into the future.

Contemporary history and past history

Who reads architectural history? And why? In his 1912–13 essay 'History and Chronicle', the Italian philosopher Benedetto Croce describes three levels of historical investment in the past: *contemporary history* (or true history), *past history* (or chronicle) and *philology* (or erudition).[5] Contemporary history tells a story that resonates with the present; it reaches forwards from the past and claims its relevance for the world of the now. This history recalls the past's lessons, and can go so far as to construct them. This is the kind of history that reminds us that things today are not vastly different from how they have ever been, that our world is the same as the world of the past. It is invoked in Burckhardt's aphorism that history 'is on every occasion the record of what one age finds worthy of note in another'.[6]

This relationship between present and past can be both benign and sinister. We might experience the past as an echo in a doorway or as a voice of authority transcending time. This contemporary history informs the historicism of all manner of cultural practices – artistic, religious, political – which look to history as more than an archive of things that have happened. Such a history is 'true' for Croce because it is the most worthy kind of history. It reaches down to the core of what he called our 'spirituality', connecting the present with its origins. When architectural history is contemporary in the sense he intended, it is a dimension of architecture's contemporaneity, its actuality.

In contrast, past history is separated from present-day life and (for Croce) man's spiritual existence. It is the history that L. P. Hartley called 'a foreign country'.[7] Whereas Croce's 'true' history has a purpose in the present, 'chronicle' is far removed from contemporary concerns. Croce explains: 'History is living chronicle, chronicle is dead history; history is contemporary history, chronicle is past history; history is principally an act of thought, chronicle is an act of will. Every history becomes chronicle when it is no longer thought, but only recorded in abstract words, which were once upon a time concrete and expressive.'[8]

This division of history from the past is not a matter of temporal but of 'spiritual' proximity, literally concerning the human spirit. Even recent history deemed to have little relevance to the present moment in any given place belongs to the category of the chronicle. He also designates as chronicles those rarefied histories of times and places long forgotten, or those monuments that, like ancient ruins, confront the viewer with a sublime sense of age and of past passed – but which offer to the present no 'lessons'.

As foreign as we ourselves might now find Croce's discussion on history, he lends us a neat conceptual division between approaches to the task of writing architectural history on the basis of the historian's relationship to a contemporary audience. Writing half a century later in *What Is History?* (1961), E. H. Carr used parallel terms to make the same point, distinguishing between 'basic' facts and 'historical' facts.[9] Insofar as it concerns architecture and its historiography, then, this distinction is not to speak of a scholarly medievalist audience for medievalist scholars. In the particular circumstances presented by architectural history, rather, a contemporary history will resonate with an audience of architects, of students of architecture, and of those others who encounter on a daily basis the problems of changing the world through building. The availability of a concept of architecture that reaches across the years and centuries is therefore important to such an audience, as it is one basis on which histories can remain poignant and relevant to architects over time. Another basis is the kind of abstraction that allows for productive misunderstandings and anachronisms, which offer lessons to the present built upon a past seen through present-day eyes and shaped by present-day values.

Consider some examples. How do the ancient structures of Assyria, the medieval architecture of Western Europe, or the buildings and dwellings of Aboriginal Australia relate to present-day architectural practice? Some would argue their fundamental relevance, on different terms and for a different geographical audience in each case. Others would consign St Stephen's Cathedral in Metz (from 1220) or the structures of Ninevah to an inert past state: obviously artful buildings, and of interest in their own terms, for scholars, but of little direct relevance to modern and contemporary architecture, with which they have almost nothing in common.

These specific cases are debatable, of course, but they serve to make a blunt point: when architectural history sets out to chronicle the past, this past architecture remains an object of study as a matter of will (as Croce suggests) rather than as a matter of import for the present. A subject is not inherently 'contemporary' or 'past'. When a subject that can be considered historically takes on a present-day importance – as Aboriginal architecture does in the light of a cultural renewal, or as Jamaica's Rastafarian architecture does within the project of its legitimization alongside conventional architecture – its status shifts from being a subject of 'dead history' to being part of a 'living chronicle'.[10] As Carr has it, 'a mere fact about the past is transformed into a fact of history.'[11] These examples are no less subject to the mechanisms of which Croce wrote a century ago than were the 'rediscovery' and romanticization of various national medieval pasts of nineteenth-century Europe. Nor are they less prone to this contemporanization than were those who in the eighteenth century 'discovered' Greece and argued the importance of its architecture for the various cultures of the Enlightenment. The fresh popularity of any given historical case or theme also belongs to this process. These diverse examples are here bound together by two connected questions. How, first of all, does the past relate to the present? And why does the present look to the past?

Contemporaneity and architectural history

These questions bring us closer to the issue of architectural history's audiences. Generally speaking, architectural history's readership can be found in the community of architectural historians as well as in the wider communities of what we can describe as architectural culture, including architects and students of architecture. Historical exhibitions expand this audience to a less specialized community, but often on the basis of even stronger claims of cultural relevance or patrimony. The imperative for new books and articles to add to and engage contemporary knowledge is therefore drawn in two directions that often diverge. A book might contribute to the disciplinary knowledge of a particular historical problem. Its readers will assess its importance for scholarship on the basis of its discoveries or its innovative analysis. The study may claim a broader significance to histories of a period, or to knowledge of a figure, or to an issue or theme that exceeds the subject to hand. A historian might regard a history as contemporary where an architect sees it as past, in these terms; or someone working within the university or the museum might see the relevance of a research theme to the problem of contemporary architectural practice where a professional architect might not immediately do so.

This clearly raises the issue of communication across disciplines and disciplinary or professional attitudes. The critical fortunes of an architectural history will depend on the cogency of the historian's argument for the significance of the details, not only to contemporary knowledge but also to contemporary problems. A book, article or exhibition might pertain to the knowledge of architectural history required by an architect for their professional practice. It could as easily relate to a more general understanding of human culture that contains lessons of broader import for contemporary culture and society.

The teaching of architectural history in professional schools of architecture presents an important institutional setting for this issue. I have knowingly conjured up a dire qualification for the content of architectural history courses, one that would have historians of architecture predict the range of historical examples, concepts and frameworks that will serve the architect as a cultured professional. Of course, someone who works constantly with the past can understand how episodes and themes in architectural history can correspond to those of present-day practice. This can partly be ascribed to a capacity for abstraction and instrumentalization that is fundamental for teaching, but it can also be understood as part of the larger and longer process by which knowledge is synthesized and reactivated over time. The pedagogy of the classroom architectural historian can be at odds with his or her activity and concerns in the field, the library or the archive.[12] Indeed, the bulk of work by architectural historians, who are commonly attached to schools of architecture, heritage agencies and museums, or departments of art history, concerns what Carr called the 'facts of the past', and often in the mode that Croce dismissed as 'dead history'. Aspects of that work can become a source for the 'true' history that would, on Croce's or Carr's terms, be the 'historical facts' of particular interest to architects as their 'contemporary history'. This qualification, then, determines the relevance – inherent or as perceived by architects and their fellow travellers of the subjects, methods, media or judgements of architectural historians.

Having posed true history as a problem, we could consider the third of Croce's historiographical categories as an antidote: 'philology' or erudition. In this context erudite history is a kind of study that privileges artefacts on their own terms, outside a relation to the present, and outside narrative structures. We could easily conjure up the stereotype of the tweed-and-elbow-patch-clad scholar working in dusty archives, books and papers piled perilously on the desk and on shelves as high as the walls allow, but we would be missing part of the point. The philologist's documents, and written artefacts especially – the term 'philology' derives from the Greek phrase for 'to love words' – are both the stuff and the complications of narrative history.

True history, as well as erudite, relies on specialized knowledge, and in architectural historiography on the agreement of buildings, monuments and other forms of architectural work with archives, libraries and other sources external to the work itself. Naturally, some who work in this mode aim to refine Carr's dead facts: revising chronologies, setting paper trails in order, questioning the involvement of one individual or another in the events to hand.

A historical study to determine the structural principles of a twelfth-century tower may shed light on a longer chronology of technical invention, on principles of what we would now call architectural composition and decoration in the medieval world, or on the various roles of the individuals involved in the conception and realization of the building. Removed from the specific imperatives of the archive, though, discoveries that could easily be dismissed as irrelevant to the twenty-first century can come to have a critical currency. When introduced as 'historical factors', they need not form a lesson, but can also act as a provocation within the field of architecture's contemporary history. In the manner that erudite history is true history's extrinsic course – extending the usefulness of Croce's terms about as far as is possible – philology lends knowledge to erudite history. This first-principles research is history's coalface, the analysis and sorting of evidence and artefacts and their reconciliation or confrontation with existing narratives. It deals in fragments rather than wholes, and as historians of recent decades in particular have learned, it can be brought to bear on the whole as a disturbance.

Proximity and distance

The slow unpacking of Croce's distinctions might seem a curiosity were the influence of his thought on history's 'spiritual' content not so fundamental to the explosion of the issue of the relationship between architectural history and architectural practice in the third quarter of the twentieth century. Particularly in the wake of the Second World War, historians of architecture demonstrated with increasing regularity that by throwing the material of the past into relief, history can be made (or found) to resonate with the present. Even if this were not the case across the entire field of architectural historiography – and it certainly was not – the post-war decades witnessed an increased tendency among architectural historians to present historically derived models for contemporary architecture and the architect, and lessons for the treatment of present-day problems faced by the architecture profession based on the path of corresponding events in the past.

The architect, therefore, is regularly the privileged reader for whom the architectural historian writes. As we have noted above, many historians are themselves trained first as architects, or consider writing or staging architectural history to be an aspect of their professional architectural practice. For the architect involved in the preservation, restoration or renovation of historic sites and buildings, the boundaries between architectural practice and historical research are only artificially enforced. Indeed, in these circumstances, the professional tenor of the historian's audience might seem an even more obvious fact. That this would pose a conceptual problem for architectural history as a disciplinary field might, conversely, seem less so. As we will briefly see below, this has over the last half-century been a subject of intense discussion, which has centred in turn on a basic point of disagreement: whether or not architectural history is written first for architects. The fundamental position taken by a historian of architecture on this issue will inform, for example, the responsibility he or she feels towards contemporary architecture as something that can be shaped by historical knowledge.

Architectural history thus shares the question of instrumentality or operativity with many branches of history. Histories of politics, warfare, economics, religion or the environment likewise regularly encounter the tendency to accept some responsibility to discover 'lessons' for an invested contemporary readership: politicians, military tacticians, economists, theologians and environmentalists. Authors might see parallels between the past and the present that become noticeable in their abstraction, or that lend new importance to old topics. This abstraction might, however, forcibly shape history so that it can inform a specific path of contemporary action on the basis of what other historians might regard as a shaky historical authority. Around this possibility circled an important post-war debate on history's usefulness to architecture.

Architecture in its history

We can approach this theme through the case of Bruno Zevi, who came to stand for, and indeed vehemently defended, a kind of instrumentalized architectural historiography. Many historians share his impassioned approach to writing on architecture and the whole-hearted enthusiasm with which he endorsed his historical 'heroes' – most famously Michelangelo, Borromini and Frank Lloyd Wright. The degree to which younger historians of architecture found his positions to be problematic becomes understandable when they are put into relief, in this case by way of a gentle reprimand by Henry A. Millon.[13] Millon would go on to become a major figure in American architectural historiography, but in 1960 he was still a doctoral student. Reacting to an editorial of Zevi's that appeared in the latter's journal *L'Architettura* (September 1957), Millon grappled with Zevi's assertions as to how useful architectural history ought to be and whether or not historians ought to try to make their history useful to architects as a matter of course – to press home its utility by conceiving of its applicability as a fundamental aspect of architectural historiography. Behind these questions lies the issue of architectural history's *proper* audience. Are these specialist histories written for specialists in architectural history? Or for scholars and students of the humanities more generally? Or for architects? Consider Millon's questions:

> Why does a man teach architectural history and how 'useful' can it be? What does the teacher hope to pass on to the student? Is history a new tool for fashioning better architects? Is history the distribution of capsules of information that will either act as a purgative to rid the student of preconceived notions, or as a vitamin to invest his designs with new vigour? Is there a direct relation between historical knowledge and architectural excellence?
>
> Or, may history be simply one of those things which aids in the maturation process of an individual, be he architect or businessman? Is it perhaps a field of study in which students learn something about themselves and others as human beings and as creators, in their greatness and their littleness? Does it perhaps instil a respect for valid achievement, a contempt for vacuous pretence, and develop the ability to discriminate between them?[14]

Millon here responds to Zevi's plea in *L'Architettura* for a form of architectural education that would make history teaching its 'backbone', subjugating all specializations of architectural education to the meta-framework of architecture's history. The teaching of construction, design, building law and so on would fall under departments of architectural history. Everyone in a school of architecture would be a critic or historian of one stripe or another, using historical knowledge as best befits their specialist subject. In this way, all architectural history would be useful, because it would help students of architecture to understand their place in time and would expose them to a plethora of worthy models and exemplars: 'Many professors', Millon quotes, 'with the most varied artistic and technical inclinations teaching only one subject: architecture in its history, acting on the problems of man in forging its modernity'.[15]

From our present-day perspective, Zevi's proposal seems quaint and naïve. Indeed, many professional architectural programmes have since moved about as far from Zevi's model as possible without abandoning the teaching of architectural history altogether. Yet it is precisely the naïvety of this pedagogical scheme that Millon addresses in his article. Zevi's idea, in abstraction, is simple and was widely endorsed in the post-war decades. There is much that history has to offer to the present, much more than can be understood by a rehearsal of the canon (against which he balked) or a relegation of history to a useless past. He takes a stance

15   Interior of the Solomon R. Guggenheim Museum, New York, by Frank Lloyd Wright, opened 1959.

against the strains of early twentieth-century modern architecture that had sought to put history to one side and which were by the 1950s beginning to exert a strong influence on American schools of architecture, themselves reacting to the tradition of the *École des beaux-arts* as it had been pursued there. He also rejected the 'cold' Germanic mode of historiography that worried away at tiny details while sacrificing the flair that was necessary for engaging students and young architects.

In his role as Chair of Architectural History at Venice, Zevi conducted 'didactic experiments' intended to test the usefulness of architectural history for future architects. Reflecting on a historical studio on the life and works of Michelangelo, he wrote in 1964 that, for a student of architecture, an encounter with architectural history and its methods would rarely lead towards a career in that specialist field.[16] The study of architectural history by architecture students would always prove fruitful, but for the most part in professional practice rather than in historical scholarship. For Zevi's students, Michelangelo shed new light on questions of artistic leadership combined with civic leadership and on invention within architectural tradition. Michelangelo had something to say about the problem of the architect-intellectual in a moment of cultural crisis, and Zevi invoked the parallels between the Second World War and the Sack of Rome as upsetting cultural norms and the artistic–architectural traditions into which they were bound.

Zevi believed in design's morality – its positive influence on families, communities, cities and nations when done well, and its disastrous impact when done badly. In turn, contemporary architecture and the problems of the design studio suggested the proper subjects of study for architectural history. Architectural historians had access to rigorous methods to which they would take recourse in studying the historical periods and figures most appropriate to their own moment. Zevi and Millon agree that the study of architectural history ought to contribute to the health of culture and society. Millon's ideas are more general, though, while Zevi's position is coloured by urgent issues of professional architectural practice and education. Zevi's views are strong, his ambitions precise.

Few architectural historians would today regard it as a bad idea to teach more architectural history to students of architecture, even if not to the extent that Zevi suggested in 1957. Studying architecture is not the same as studying architectural history. With this in mind, Millon closes with an apposite observation: 'the real danger to the student is from the historian who strips down or soups up his presentation to get a little more mileage out of the Art Nouveau or the Space Frame. Denatured or over-vitalised presentations will give the alert student architectural indigestion, while a spirited, sincere exposition by a competent scholar may offer sustaining nourishment.'[17]

Stripped down, souped up or straight up?

While this virtual discussion between Millon and Zevi is just one episode in the history of this question, by reading their articles we can see two basic positions at work, against which we can consider the broader issue of the utility of knowledge of the past to the practice of architecture. It is worthwhile to recall that among the historiographical traditions from which a modern, academic architectural history emerged at the end of the nineteenth century, one concerned the knowledge of the past considered by architects as their professional and artistic patrimony. To what degree, then, are architectural historians today obliged to attend to the audience of a contemporary professional architectural culture?

Another reaction to Zevi's ideas on the issue of the historian's audience can help us to further probe into this issue. In a notoriously ungenerous reading, Tafuri observes that Zevi wanted, through history, to make architecture and the architect more important to contemporary society than they had, in his view, proved themselves to be. His conception, though, of the challenges architecture faced in the post-war world, the solutions the architect could offer, and the historical knowledge necessary to build a bridge from post-war reality to a brighter future was so blinkered as to be of no use to his cause.[18] Zevi's architectural history was critically charged, and his criticism (in *L'Architettura*) full of historical cases and allusions. Those cases, though, gave rise to what

Tafuri called 'false hopes', which offered a poor reconciliation of historical knowledge with historical narrative. For
Zevi's insistence, though, on seeing the problems of the
present foreshadowed in those of the past, Croce could have
no better example of the 'true architectural historian'.

Under Zevi's historiographical regime, the historian would
follow the lead of the architect, who would understand the
problems of contemporary society and architecture's place
therein, and then take over: presenting good, relevant history
and editing out bad and irrelevant examples. One would no
longer need to think about second-rate, minor or peripheral
architects, however important historians might find them
beyond their application to present-day problems. Why
bother? Effective architectural history better educates architects and prepares society for the better architecture they will
build and the better cities they will plan. The historian of this
stripe would, therefore, not simply study materials and issues
that were of pure, rarefied, scholarly interest, but would test
their choice of subject against present needs. Architectural
history, therefore, is that portion of knowledge of the past
that remains relevant. This is the measure of any given historical subject's legitimacy.

Tafuri argued against this approach, but to the same ends.
How can the architect know what in architectural history is
worthy of study if he or she only knows a small portion of
that history? Even if a historian of architecture makes that
choice from a broad field of historical knowledge, the nature
of transmission means that those geographies, cultures, architects and epochs edited out on the grounds of irrelevance are
lost to subsequent generations. Tafuri claimed that a strong
sense of 'internal' historical authority and continuity allowed
architecture to become isolated from society. Rather than
providing the architect with easy answers drawn from the
past, Tafuri thought, architectural historians ought to recall
the messiness surrounding the way buildings are made, and
to remind present-day readers of cases, architects and problems that fell out of view for being at odds with architecture's
neater histories. As Tafuri would have it in rebuttal of
Zevi's position, the architectural historian studied the past
in order to present historical knowledge with no 'aesthetic
conclusion'.[19]

16 Still from *Le mani sulla città*, directed by Federico Rosi (1963).

This might seem counter-intuitive: how would *not* helping architects to understand history in present-day terms make them better architects? Tafuri's answer lay in the unexpected lessons and resonances of the past, which architects would find in histories that were meant to be not useful but provocative, undermining the common values of architecture derived from historical abstractions such as Zevi advanced. The consequences of architects reading history would be unpredictable from the historian's point of view, but this itself would be a sign of the profession's health, and of its ability to identify and attend to the problems of society. Rather than helping architects to form useful habits (Zevi), architectural historians would help to prevent architects from designing out of habit (Tafuri).

This distinction gives rise to two loosely organized but persistent schools of thought on how useful architectural history ought to be for architecture. Zevi considered architectural history as architectural practice by other means. Tafuri thought that architectural historians should write architectural history and architects should know what to do

with it. Both ideas of architectural history would be underpinned by a knowledge of architecture equivalent to that held
by the architect, but each position on the architectural historian's role in relation to the architect assumes a greater or
lesser distance from the exigencies of the office and studio.

Cultural versus architectural instrumentalization

These discussions allow us to home in on three positions that
continue to shape the terms under which architectural history
is deemed 'useful' to its professional audience. Zevi's is the
contextualist position for which history is one of many settings determining the architect's approach to composition,
planning, decoration, materials and so forth. Second, drawing
from Millon's response, is a tempered version of the same
stance: architectural history has much to teach us – architects
and accountants alike – but architectural knowledge is hardly
limited by history's structures and abstractions. Third, Tafuri
takes the critical stance: the historian of architecture can act
against the habits upheld by architectural history, and this
antagonism can in turn question the facts concerning historical models, referents and precedents. As such, these positions
describe three stances that could variously be considered
disciplinary or habitudinal: architecture within history, for
architecture (Zevi); architecture alongside history, for culture
(Millon); and history against architecture, for architecture
(Tafuri).

The warning implied in this analysis is not far removed
from another offered by Carr. He writes of the undergraduate 'recommended to read a work by that great scholar Jones
of St. Jude's' who wisely asks a friend at St Jude's 'what sort
of chap Jones is, and what bees he has in his bonnet'. Architectural histories written with a professional readership of
architects in mind will not only be aware of their readers'
technical and artistic expertise, but they will recognize that
their readers also design works of architecture that will one
day become the material of the past and perhaps, depending
upon the qualifications, the matter of architectural history.
This awareness is inevitably underpinned by an idea of the
historian's role in architectural culture that gives way to a

historiographical agenda, which Carr describes as the 'buzzing' of the bees in the historian's bonnet. 'If you can detect none', he writes, 'either you are tone deaf or your historian is a dull dog'.[20]

One of the architectural historian's most important tasks is to understand and appraise the past, to recover decisions and guess at their consequences. In this sense, architectural historiography explores the relationship between historical formation and perspective and the construction, defence and criticism of a historical corpus of architectural knowledge. The meaning of all of these terms is open to debate, and through this debate the limits of the discipline or field or specialization of architectural history are received, tested and defended from moment to moment. In this light, we might restate the three positions described earlier through Zevi, Millon and Tafuri in relation to three specific stances relative to the corpus of historical knowledge of architecture, the content of architectural history: instrumental historiography as the manipulation of historical knowledge, scientific or learned history as the study of architectural history for its own ends, and critical history as the use of knowledge and analysis against history's manipulation to ends direct (instrumental and operative) or habitual (resulting from pervasive hegemonies). Just as many schemas advanced thus far in this book are merely diagrams of tendencies rather than entire approaches, architectural historians will more often than not affiliate with one of these positions in concert with aspects of the others.

The degree to which any one *attitude* towards writing architectural history is given greater licence to shape architectural history (its frames, perspectives, objectives and effects) depends to a large extent on the author's or the curator's concept of their audience and of the immediate importance of his or her history for that audience. The direction of one's instrumentalization, it stands to reason, is a vital aspect of this problem. It is useful to make a distinction between the advancement of culture, in which architecture and the architect take part, and the advancement of architecture per se, as a question of form, theory, plan and meaning. The form of architectural history that might seem contemporary for one of these ambitions might seem dead for the other. The latter of these two ambitions promoted a form of historical instrumentalization against which many historians and theoreticians of architecture have taken a critical stance since the 1970s. Their reaction gave rise to a critical historiographical tradition loosely connected with Tafuri's ambitions for his discipline that set out to antagonize the Western canon and to question its importance for contemporary architecture. This development lent an altogether different character to the more recent study of architectural history.

5
History and theory

Problems in historicizing architecture

So far in this book, we have considered several different origins for modern architectural historiography. The disciplinary field we have considered is one that emerged, in part, at the end of the nineteenth century from the systematic study of architectural history within the rubric of cultural history. As it did so, it encountered the increasingly formalized teaching of architectural history in professional schools and academies of architecture. We have treated the problems of this modern field of architectural history as three-dimensional, involving the interplay of frameworks and approaches, materials and evidence, and audience. Other formulae might have worked just as well, or better, but this approach has allowed us to make two basic points at some length. The first is that the shifting definitions of architecture, historical and contemporary, have shaped the content of architectural history and the methods of its analysis. The second is that architectural history draws a crucial aspect of its legitimization as a field of research and teaching from architectural practice, the present-day exigencies of architecture, and the demands of an architect-readership.

This does not mean that architectural history is inevitably prone to anachronism. Many historians of architecture work precisely against this tendency by recovering, in the modes of Croce's critical philology or Tafuri's critical historiography, the historical conditions under which buildings, monuments and city precincts were conceived, negotiated and realized in past moments. Neither does it imply that architectural history is inevitably in the service of professional interests and the programmatic imperatives of architecture itself. Many architectural historians are indeed trained first as professional architects; as a result, many hold topics of architectural history up against the needs of contemporary practice as a qualification for their study, or demand that historical analysis is brought directly to bear on issues of the present. There are, however, strong and important disciplinary counter-traditions, the most significant of which being the study of architectural history within the history of art, within social, institutional, and intellectual history, and as a subject for the close study of architecture's documentary landscape.

In the twenty-first century, as in the nineteenth, architectural history stands before a set of conceptual problems derived from these sometimes contradictory institutional and intellectual traditions from which it emerged and to which it has to varying degrees been held accountable. This situation is shared by other histories of professions, arts and techniques, like music, for example, or medicine, where a historical discipline has formed alongside an art's or a profession's consciousness of its historical patrimony.

Among its roles, architectural history serves to define the historical context of contemporary architecture. To this extent it must negotiate, articulate or reconcile the differences between what architecture is, what it has been and, for some, what it can or ought to be. The term 'architecture' has sometimes allowed accidental conflations of past and present realities and perspectives for historians and architects alike. This is, of course, a fundamental issue for all branches of history: how to know the past in the present. It is made slightly more pressing in architectural history, however, because extant works of historical architecture acquire contemporary significance and are known within contemporary modes of visuality and experience. A building of the seventeenth century that remains standing today is not past in a simple sense. The complexity of this situation feeds back into the analysis of the stock of historical architecture, however defined, into the history of architectural ideas, and into the terms of reference for knowing architecture as a historically situated practice.

As we noted above, there are many possible views on the historical field that remains plausibly connected to architecture as it is known now. Some follow the trajectory of Tafuri's *Progetto e utopia*, Peter Collins's *Changing Ideals in Modern Architecture* (1965), Joseph Rykwert's *The First Moderns* (1980) and Kenneth Frampton's *Modern Architecture* (1980), each of which locates the origins of contemporary architecture in developments of the eighteenth century, Enlightenment thinking, the diminishing importance of the classical tradition, and the rise of aesthetics.[1] Historiographically, though, this can give rise to a complex mid-past comprising the eighteenth and nineteenth centuries and a flattened-out deep-past made up of the centuries preceding this relatively cohesive periodization. It ties the history of modern architecture to the intellectual developments that oversaw the rise of architectural history.

Critical architectural history

The generation of architectural historians who became prominent in the 1960s and 1970s reacted against the identification of architectural history with the values of architectural modernism that could be found in the books of Pevsner, Giedion and Zevi. If the modern movement had fulfilled a series of promises contained in those histories, then what, they asked, was left either to history or to architecture as architectural modernism began to fade and crack as an ideological endpoint? Banham, Tafuri, Robert Venturi and others of their generation expressed disappointment in the path taken by modern architecture in the post-war decades, and realigned the tasks of history with those of, again, contemporary architecture. Questions of form and function gave way to others of historicity and meaning.

The audience for the history written in this period commonly described this work as architectural theory. Theory, in this sense, no longer stood for the operating rules of architectural practice. Historically, architectural theory had been the means of intellectualizing the rules of architectural composition, disposition, materials, ornamentation and so forth – thinking through architecture's borders as an art, discipline, profession or craft. This is the theory tracked by the wide-ranging surveys of Kruft and Mallgrave, noted earlier. From the 1960s, theory came to define the more open critico-historical analysis of architecture. It was postmodern in the sense defined by Lyotard.[2] It set aside grand narratives and opened the door to an increasingly relativized knowledge. In architecture this intellectual shift combined semiotic theory (of a kind), historical revisionism, and Freudo-Marxist perspectives on architecture, its history and historiography. By the 1980s it further welcomed a translation of the deconstructive philosophy given widespread currency by Jacques Derrida in his 1967 book *De la grammatologie.*[3] Architecture's later-twentieth-century intellectual history presents a curious confusion of terms.[4] The reactions to anachronistic and teleological architectural historiography mounted in the 1960s and 1970s and given full expression in the 1980s and 1990s rejected the subservience of architectural history to architectural theory, of a critical point of view to projective thinking. It did so, however, in the language of a critical history, (now) understood as a manifestation of 'theory' as a genre of humanities writing.[5]

The work of many architectural historians active from the 1960s onwards was shaped by shifts in tone and value across the humanities disciplines. Especially was this the case in anglophone settings of humanities study, particularly in North America, which rose to dominance during these decades. This was due, not least, to the innovative adaptation and dissemination of continental philosophy carried out by American scholars of architecture, but also to basic changes in the institutional structures supporting their work, like the emergence of the Ph.D. in architecture and the dramatically expanded programmes of key publishers of books and journals in the history and theory of architecture. The intellectual, stylistic and institutional changes tracked by these developments did not, however, see a corresponding change to the fundamental questions posed of the architectural historian's place in architectural culture. Ultimately, the nature of this issue did not differ substantially between modernist historians and the critical historians who followed them, even if the place of criticism, history and other forms of intellectualization and reflection in architectural culture was more secure than it had ever been. In this light, consider the questions posed by Anthony Vidler in *Histories of the Immediate Present*:

> What, in short, does the architectural historian do, not qua history, but for architects and architecture? Or, to put it more theoretically, What kind of work does or should architectural history perform for architecture, and especially for contemporary architecture? This of course is a version of the commonplace refrain, How is history 'related' to design? Is it *useful*? And if so, in what ways?[6]

The last of Vidler's questions directly recalls the discussions documented in the previous chapter, but we can pull the question of utility in a different direction. The kind of usefulness we considered above invoked the possibilities of a direct relationship between history and theory. Should the architectural historian work with an eye on the future? Was the objective of architectural history the distillation of models and rules for the contemporary practice of architecture? Should history, that is, nudge architecture into the future? Vidler surveys the writing of several historians of art and architecture who thought that, yes, history should serve these roles. One could intellectualize the past as a historian, and historicize contemporary architecture, but the ends were programmatic. Truly modern history was in tune with the *Zeitgeist*. It aided the production of modern architecture because it was synchronized with the most progressive expressions of the age. By the 1970s and 1980s, this form of historiography was widely thought to be decidedly *passé*.

The often artificial distinctions between architectural history and architectural theory made since the 1970s have regularly reflected a difference in historiographical values rather than a basic difference between one mode of enquiry and another. Vidler's post-war cases (Rowe, Banham, Tafuri) occasionally profile as theoreticians. Other times, they present as critics and historians. When they are theoreticians, they are not so in the sense that differentiates antagonistically from history. And when they are historians, they exhibit the criticality characterizing the theory-work of that moment. Indeed, they tread a line that defines critical architectural history: that theorized history of architecture, its intellectual content and its representation; and that historicized theorization of the same. It fulfils the criteria of theory as a reflective and self-reflective postmodern academic writing genre without converting historical analysis into architectural programme.

Vidler is himself a major figure of architecture's 'theory moment'. His attention, since the late 1990s, to the history of architectural historiography is a natural extension of its project. More recently, critical history-as-theory has tended to 'concretize' as a form of intellectual history-after-theory concerned with a broadly defined architectural culture. The emergence of the subgenre of the history of architectural historiography is symptomatic of a desire to understand the transition from the sureties of modernism and the modernist project to the absolute relativity of all knowledge in the prelude to, and then wake of, the deconstructive turn in the humanities.

Building on such examples as Kruft's history of architectural theory and the intellectual biography of Giedion written by Sokratis Georgiadis (1989), the history of architectural historiography had by the end of the 1990s become a mainstream discourse for architectural historians.[7] Books on a number of historians and intellectuals of architectural culture came to assume an important place in architectural history. Despite widespread objections that this work moved architectural historians away from architecture as the discipline's centre, it became both legitimate and popular to treat the intellectual history of architecture's broader cultural and intellectual make-up, and thus to write of historical architecture through its historians. These developments saw the canon return to centre-stage, but mediated by the study of historiography and historiology. This history of architecture as the history of architectural history and the history of architectural ideas attended to a definition of architecture as a discourse.

We can understand these developments historically according to recent thinking about the ambitions and strategies of the humanities more generally at the end of the twentieth century. Ian Hunter describes this moment as follows:

> Unlike natural scientific theories, the theory that emerged in the humanities and social sciences in the 1960s was not defined by its object because it surfaced in disciplines with quite divergent objects: linguistics and legal studies, literature and anthropology, the study of folktales and the analysis of economic modes of production. Further, the theoretical vernaculars that emerged at this time differed significantly, sometimes in accordance with the university faculties where theorists were employed, but also in accordance with divergent (or only partially overlapping) national intellectual contexts.[8]

When Vidler asks, then, 'What kind of work does or should architectural history perform for architecture, and especially for contemporary architecture?', he raises a question with deep repercussions for the organization of architectural history among what have more recently and more generously been termed (principally in Britain) the 'architectural humanities' – the history, theory and criticism of architecture as a broad category of intellectual and analytical activities that gravitate, though not exclusively, to curatorial, editorial and written expression. This has naturally impacted on the ambitions and tenor of many forms of architectural historiography and on the intellectual and institutional possibilities available to the historian of architecture.

What is architectural history and theory?

Iain Borden uses a telling conjugation in the *Bartlett Book of Ideas* when he asks, 'What is Architectural History and Theory?' He places this humanities arm of architecture firmly in the realm of 'theory' when he writes, 'Architecture becomes a provisional entity, held out for preliminary inspection like the fly caught in a spider's web, only to be captured again with every new dawn. Architecture becomes certain and unknown, and herein lies its beauty. . . . And through a self-conscious reflection on this process, architectural history and theory must in turn be similarly subjected to equal re-examination.'[9] This is architecture's contribution to the form of the theory that Terry Eagleton wrote of as 'critical self-reflection . . . Theory of this kind comes about when we are forced into a new self-consciousness about what we are doing.'[10] When we follow Vidler's cue and ask what 'work' architectural history does, or did, we are also asking how it participated in this theoretical moment as an expression of disciplinary or epistemological self-consciousness. How did critical history-as-theory serve architectural culture in this moment of (sometimes extreme) relativization and (often dense, even impenetrable) textual production? How did the interdisciplinary dissemination of critical theory shape its historiographical production – and the 'work' done by architectural history for architecture?

Although widespread and influential, this development was not universal. Many architectural historians resisted architecture's turn to theory, offering a firm ground for those pursuing the scientific study of architectural history that was regarded as obstinate and naïve by those of the theory camp. Some openly declared this theory moment as transitory and refused to engage with its whimsies. Others recognized the theorist-historian's tools from the older traditions of philology and the cultural sciences. It is in the nature of this resistance not to be explicit about methods and perspectives, but to focus on the subject at hand. The dust-jacket copy of Christoph L. Frommel's *Architecture of the Italian Renaissance* (2007) is nevertheless symptomatic of this latter insistence on a solid approach to architectural history.[11] His publishers present the book by observing, 'Avoiding the straitjacket of fashionable theory, this book is organized traditionally by period and architect. Social context, technical innovation and aesthetic judgement are all given due weight.' We ought not to read too much into this statement. Frommel's position is not, after all, conservative in the sense that non-theoretical histories were regularly held to be across recent decades. He rather intimates the security with which he views the tools of his discipline and their limitations. Despite the high profile and often-privileged status of theorized architectural history in the 1980s and 1990s, the persistence of architectural historians like Frommel and institutions like the Bibliotheca Hertziana, for which he once served as Director, gave post-theory historians of architecture something to return to, and a-theoretical historians something to cling to.

We are, of course, presenting a complex and often subtle set of negotiations over definitions, methods and ambitions as a series of somewhat crude camps. Many examples that come to mind undermine them, but they do serve to isolate some of the tendencies of this time. The historical moment of theory, like all those distinguishable episodes of architectural historiography preceding it, was given a different expression by different linguistic groups and national and regional debates in the field. For all the differences we might invoke, however, it had a 'shared intellectual attitude or deportment'.[12] The most dominant discourse of the last quarter of the twentieth century, which informed that 'attitude or deportment' more thoroughly than any other, was staged on the northeast coast of the United States, in and around 'theory's natural home: the American humanities graduate school'.[13] During the 1970s, this setting opened a door to America's graduate schools of architecture, which decisively shaped the direction of theory production from that time onwards. For its influence over the recent directions of architectural history, this institutional history deserves our brief attention.

Institutional corollaries

The introduction of the Doctor of Philosophy (Ph.D.) degree in American schools of architecture was an important step in architecture's participation in the theory moment. The first American Ph.D. programmes in architecture were developed by the University of Pennsylvania and the University of California–Berkeley. The formation in 1975 of the Ph.D. in the History, Theory and Criticism of Architecture and Art at the Massachusetts Institute of Technology – within America's oldest university school of architecture – signalled a change to this institutional landscape. Under the guidance of Stanford Anderson and Henry A. Millon, architecture faculty and graduate students alike sought to intellectualize architecture and its history on terms that ensured the full participation of architecture in the wider development of the critical humanities.[14] Before this moment in the United States, graduate study in architectural history was largely the domain of the Ph.D. in the discipline of art history, where it has continued to be taught, and where it has likewise contributed to this same intellectual project. Especially has this been the case in the art history departments of the University of California at Los Angeles, Cornell University and Columbia University. MIT has graduated a number of influential figures in American architectural history and theory since the early 1980s, as have the graduate art history and (more recently) architecture programmes of UCLA, UC Berkeley, Columbia, Cornell, and Harvard. Other key university centres for architectural theory in the United States included Princeton and Yale universities, the Cooper Union and a number of important state universities – particularly Iowa, where Jennifer Bloomer and Catherine Ingraham conducted influential research on architectural representation.

Individuals based in these various universities – and other besides – together worked on the formation of a discourse exploring architecture's limits as a setting and provocation for the interdisciplinary study of architecture and its history in the mode of theory. Across the Atlantic, the Architectural Association and Cambridge University similarly formed important British sites for architecture's participation in the humanities theory moment, and as many of the key figures of these decades were regularly present in the important centres of the American northeast, so too were they often found in Bedford Square or Scroop Terrace.

This lens on the intellectual developments in architecture is admittedly rather narrow. It does not follow the trajectory of intellectualized architectural history across Europe – in Paris, Barcelona, Delft, Berlin, Zurich, Venice and other key continental centres of architectural thought – as well as in anglophone settings that resisted the work of an American-style architectural theory. The international attention to the American theory centres was, however, so strong as to regularly draw those thinkers, categorized as theorists or theoreticians, into discussions that were American in setting, European in outlook, and regularly replete with an international range of accents.

Jean-Louis Cohen has observed that the interpretation of French philosophy, for instance, by Italian writers of architectural history theory in the 1960s and 1970s introduced French critical theory to a French architecture audience who in the 1970s became attentive to the work of Italian thinkers.[15] The translation of those Italian books and articles into English, and the systematic uptake of post-structuralist French philosophy in the pages of various books and journals, further aided the introduction of critical theory to architectural history and theory. There is, naturally, a parallel history of the reception in architectural theory of German-language philosophy and critical theory through international translation and transmission. (The small but influential political journal *Contropiano* regularly published articles on architecture and cities that explored the implications of a range of German and Austrian thinkers for architectural knowledge. Beatriz Colomina has observed how Spanish readers received these articles in translation, drawing upon them to cultivate a politicized theoretical production on architectural themes, especially in Barcelona under the influence of Ignasi de Solà-Morales.[16]) The assimilation of French philosophy by Tafuri and his Italian contemporaries into a critical architectural history and a history of architectural ideas, suggests Cohen, introduced philosophical systems to French architectural culture, which had not explored the possibilities, for architectural thinking, of structuralist and later post-structuralist philosophy.

During these decades many ideas originating in continental philosophy, literature, politics, mathematics, economics and history were thoroughly mined for their architectural implications, and as a result were often drastically transformed.[17]

Outside the university, the (recently reinstated[18]) Institute for Architecture and Urban Studies (IAUS) in New York was, from 1967 to 1985, a crucial clearinghouse of international theory. Its roll of fellows, variously under the direction of Peter Eisenman, Mario Gandelsonas, Anthony Vidler and Steven Peterson, included a number of critical historians whose work was viewed as theory, and several theoreticians and architects whose material was historical. In the former camp we can count Kenneth Frampton and Rosalind Krauss, and in the latter Diana Agrest, Rafael Moneo and Rem Koolhaas. Its journal *Oppositions* surveyed the limits of architectural theory and critical architectural history as written in a theoretical genre. It published essays by the aforementioned directors and fellows, as well as work by a vast number of international guests including a series of books, Oppositions Books, published by MIT Press.[19] It tracked the shift from interest in semiotics and post-structuralism to the first salvos in the 1980s of architectural deconstructionism and deconstructivism – as a historiographical strategy and stance and as a programmatic architectural theory of formal invention and deformation.

Teresa Stoppani[20] has recently observed the importance of the IAUS to what we could call the second generation of American architectural theorists for bridging Tafuri's mode of critical architectural history – celebrated in the term 'Venice School' – and the architectural-theory discourse that opened the field of architecture itself well beyond the realm of building, valorizing as the material of architectural history an exponentially expanding field: from literary sources, film and music, to popular media and ephemera, to philosophical concepts with an architectural resonance, to architectural concepts with philosophical implications, and so on. If it could be brought to bear on or be made to express architectural problems or themes, it could readily be legitimated as the material of this new theorized critical history. Bloomer's *Architecture and the Text* (1993) and the essays of Joel Sanders's *Stud* (1996) are good examples of an open approach to the methods, evidence and political project of criticism and historiography in architectural culture.[21]

Under K. Michael Hays and Catherine Ingraham, the journal *Assemblage* staged the work of many of this second generation of architectural theory's protagonists. The journal's final issue, number 41 (2000), presents a series of one-page, state-of-the-question contributions from each of the writers who had published in the journal since its first issue (1987), and who could now look back on this period with a measure of hindsight. It is interesting, from a historical point of view, how *Assemblage* 41 documents an uncertainty in the ongoing relevance of architecture's theory-project as it had been conceived and implemented in the last years of the twentieth century.[22] The conclusion of this journal hardly marked an end to architectural theory, or to theorized history, any more than had the theory moment marked an end to philology or to a narrative, canonical approach to architectural historiography. Indeed, in 2007 Hays defended the ongoing relevance of critical theory for the architectural historian, writing: 'The more theory, the more access to history. Theory is the practice that produces concepts and categories to map the Real of History.'[23]

The lessons of theory

Speaking in the broadest of terms, we can think of developments in the architectural humanities of recent decades, and especially as they were manifested in North America and Britain, as a shift to greater relativity, enabling a deeper level of auto-critique and self-reflection. Speaking just as broadly, we might think of the present moment as one witnessing a diminishing relativity among historians, critics and theoreticians, whereby the chain of theory-as-critique-of-teleological-history gave way to theory-for-theory's-sake, which has in turn allowed the more recent iteration of history-to-overcome-theory. Architectural historians have seen the reinstatement of the building and its documentary trail as the ground-plane of their work, although the relative innocence of pre-theory-moment historiography has been lost. No one can speak of the canon without qualification; no one can write of the Western tradition of architecture without condition. The possibilities of a critical philology – the close study of documents, the increased importance of fine details – have come into clearer focus.

This is not merely as a return to earlier forms of historical analysis, but also as an extension of the ambitions of critical architectural historiography beyond the specific form lent it by the theory moment. These general shifts in attitudes and intentions, such as can be traced at the conferences of SAH, SAHANZ or Britain's Architectural Humanities Research Association, or in the pages of the *Journal of Architecture* and the *JSAH*, might seem odd to those who ushered in the freedoms of the 1980s and 1990s. They might also seem a long time coming to those who ignored those freedoms and their attendant relativization. For those harbouring the most extreme attitudes to this recent and, for some, traumatic institutional and intellectual history, the separation between theory and post-theory will appear as an impossible chasm. It nevertheless remains possible for us to identify a series of historiographical themes and attitudes that owe a debt to architecture's theory moment, even if they now belong to what has been construed, in terms of equal contingency, as a 'return to history'.

As much as we can speak of a 'return' to architectural history, we must recognize that it is neither easy nor simple. Critical theory has allowed historians to make fundamental insights into the workings and representation of knowledge and the conditions of its production and survival. Architectural history and its production have by no means been exempt from these lessons. Historians working more recently, who have some experience of these intellectual developments, but who turn again to what might be called architectural history's 'core' concerns, are well aware of the implications of this intellectual history for their research, writing and teaching in the present. Books by Reinhold Martin and Felicity Scott, who with Branden Joseph edit the journal *Grey Room* (founded 2000), demonstrate the possibilities of such a history.[24] The increased weight given recently to the intellectualization of architectural history itself – the historians and their values – is symptomatic of the effects of a sustained spell of theoretical reflection on the disciplinary field and its relation to architectural culture.

A long roll call of architectural historians has been subject to this kind of analysis, from the scholars of Vienna and Venice to the founders of American, British, Turkish, South African, Iberian, French, Belgian, Italian, Australasian and other national or regional historiographical communities. This examination is inevitably couched in the search for and analysis of disciplinary models. (When the subjects of this intellectual historiography confront us with unconscionable political views, such as the generation of art historians sympathetic with the aims of German National Socialism, understanding their cases historically has helped us to see how the ideas that shape historical research can themselves relinquish the basic conditions of civilization that its historians appear to defend.)[25] Much of this research and scholarship takes up

Carr's exhortation to know the historian before knowing the history. By studying the historians of architecture we would understand how historiographical devices have shaped the history of architecture and thus the historical architectural subject in the present.

Other critical studies of contemporary architecture have demonstrated how historical cases might operate under a broader rubric of criticality in architectural culture, where the present can inform knowledge of the past against the activation of that knowledge to ends determined by architectural programme. The critico-historical writing to appear in more recent issues of *Thresholds* (founded 1992) are examples of this. So too are those contributions to *Log* (founded in 2003), the journal which grew out of the ANY project of the 1990s directed by Cynthia Davidson from 1993 to 2000: a series of internationally staged and staffed events and publications exploring criticality within architectural theory. So, too, although in a different tenor, is the historical typological research published and presented by Momoyo Kaijima and Yoshiharu Tsukamoto of Atelier Bow-Wow.[26] Behind these approaches and others like them is a productive but relentless examination and cross-examination of the field of architecture by architectural historians we can describe as critical and theoretical.

Postcolonial architectural history is likewise a strong force to emerge from these intellectual, institutional and historical circumstances of the 1990s. Its terms have informed the historiography of a vast number of geographies and cultures, and its effect has been to both broaden and deepen the definition of 'architecture' by divorcing it from the last vestiges of the unquestioned Western canon.[27] It maps a historical enquiry concerned with the ways in which the power, forces and habits of subjugation shape the production and the analysis of architecture. This has given rise to themes that are as theoretical as they are historical: flows of political power, influence, patronage and privilege; economics, politics, ideology; gender, sexuality and race; mentality, collective memory, worldview, representation, psychology. These themes have come to stand for a persistent awareness that the past of architectural history is no closed book. The recent theorization and historicization of the preservation and restoration

17 Façade, new Post Office, Algiers, Algeria, early twentieth century.

of buildings and city precincts offers a further reminder of this lesson. The American journal *Future Anterior* (established 2004) explores the complex interactions between history-as-knowledge and heritage-as-trace that have been recognized through the theorization of the way that historical architecture endures in the present *and* of the way that this work has acquired and retained historical significance.

The precise means of this insistently critical and doggedly suspicious analysis of architecture's past is hardly limited by the scope of pre-theory historiography as a backdrop for present-day disciplinary efforts. The adaptation of tools and approaches of other disciplines has been a source of productive interference for architectural historians, for whom parallel historical specializations, continental philosophy, the theorization of politics, economics, corporations and systems, technology and the sciences have offered surprising insights into traditional and canonical subjects of architectural history. For all of these reasons the canon has not exactly

18   Oath of Office Ceremony (2009) at the US Air Force Academy, Colorado Springs, Colorado, with the Chapel by Skidmore, Owens & Merrill (1962) depicted in the background.

disappeared. Its content has set an important test for those tools and approaches developed and adapted to address new challenges and expectations posed of knowledge by the humanities and their many settings.

In the final analysis, the building poses a specific challenge to cultural knowledge to which the research and teaching of architectural historians has long been addressed. What knowledge, they ask, is embedded in the building? What accrues in the building by virtue of where and when it exists? How does the building shed light on the past? And how does it exist as a trace of the past? These are persistent questions that remain at the core of the architectural historian's enquiry.

What then?

The picture I have painted of architectural history and historiography is that of a modern disciplinary field and practice. As much as architectural history assumes the behaviour, form and structure of a discipline, it borrows persistently and extensively from its cognate fields and, more recently, from less predictable sources of knowledge, material, analytical strategies and media. Across the humanities, disciplines are vastly different now from their forms of half a century ago. It follows that as a body of knowledge, an evidentiary field and a set of tools and assumptions, the work of architectural historians today would by and large be unrecognizable to Heinrich Wölfflin and disconcerting to Sigfried Giedion; it might appear nonsensical to Geoffrey Scott and frayed to Henri Focillon.

As an abstract endeavour, the project of knowing architecture's past in terms that reconcile the intrinsic and often unrecoverable facts of any given subject, be it a building, a drawing, a life-in-architecture, with the qualifications that allow it to interest scholars in the present has changed little across the decades. Architecture remains a profession for some historians, an art for others, and a cultural mirror for others still. As we have seen, few historians would treat the history of architecture from one perspective, disciplinary or methodological, without introducing a degree of balance. Now, as in the past, this has enriched architectural historiography as a practice. As a practice and a field of knowledge, it remains shaped by forces, weak and strong, which are subject to reappraisal now more than ever before. Indeed, the subject and work of architectural historians is open to a constant test of boundaries, methods, materials, and even the position of architectural history relative to the wider cultural and institutional settings of architecture.

The metropolitan, regional, national and international scales at which the Office of Metropolitan Architecture (OMA) and its research-twin AMO practise under the firm hand of Koolhaas have insisted on new terms for the architect's work, which has helped to shape architecture's contemporary agenda. The tools of architecture, their work argues, can shape governance, capital, consumerism and national and continental identities. Their claim separates the media of architectural practice from its tools and strategies. As a result, the terms of architectural historiography have also begun to shift. How can the tools and strategies of architectural historiography inform the analysis and implications of histories of government, law, politics, consumption, religion, nationalism and so forth? Reinhold Martin's 'Think Tank'[28] studio at Columbia University confronts these questions, as did the working conference 'Aggregate'[29] organized by John Harwood at Oberlin College (April 2008), and Eyal Weizman's analyses of Israel and Palestine.[30] In short, architecture's present-day professional and cultural brief is wide-ranging, and we can find consequences of this in architectural history's scope.

What is the shape of the present-day situation for architectural history, historiography, historiology and historians? In the final analysis this is impossible to say without the possibility of taking a critical distance from the disciplinary and institutional situation of the present moment. The field has undergone dramatic reassessment in recent decades, but will these changes exceed those introduced at the end of the nineteenth century? Will their effects be more acutely felt, or more strongly defended? In the conclusion to his article 'Notes on Narrative Method in Historical Interpretation', Hays suggests that 'the practice of writing [architectural history]... would be a force that thickens the situation, slows thinking down'.[31] At a time when architecture's remit appears to be ever-expanding, and when criticism and criticality in architecture enjoy a greater mobility than ever before, this persistent disciplinary agenda might well continue to present the most relevant, if challenging, path for the present-day field of architectural history.

Notes

Introduction

1 Heinrich Wölfflin, *Renaissance and Baroque*, trans. Kathrin Simon (London: Collins, 1964), xi. Originally as *Renaissance und Barock: Eine Untersuchung über Wesen und Entstehung des Barockstils in Italien* (Munich: T. Ackerman, 1888).

2 The Getty Research Institute (Los Angeles), the Center for Advanced Studies in the Visual Arts at the National Gallery (Washington, DC), the Canadian Center for Architecture (Montreal), the Sterling and Francine Clark Institute (Williamstown, Mass.) and the Institut National d'Histoire de l'Art (Paris) are among the major research institutions hosting programmes in the history of art and architecture, and which publish the work of their researchers. The Bibliotheca Hertziana in Rome is a key library for the study of architectural history as are those of the Centro Internazionale di Studi di Architettura (CISA) 'Andrea Palladio' at Vicenza; the Villa I Tatti of Harvard University, near Florence; the Centre d'Études Supérieures de la Renaissance at Tours; the Stiftung Bibliothek Werner Oechslin in Einsiedeln; the Warburg Institute at London; and a number of other significant university collections. This list is hardly complete, but indicates the range of settings for scholarly research in the history of architecture.

3 Giulio Lorenzetti, *Venezia e il suo estuario. Guida storico-artistica* (Venice: Bestetti & Tumminelli, 1926); Engl. edn, *Venice and its Lagoon*, trans. John Guthrie (Padua: Edizioni

Erredici, 2002); for the full catalogue and history of what are now called The Pevsner Architectural Guides, see www. pevsner.co.uk; on the Buildings of the United States, see the website of the Society of Architectural Historians (SAH), www.sah.org/index.php?submenu=Publications&src=gendocs &ref=BUS&category=Publications.

4 The American Society (later just the Society) of Architectural Historians was established in 1941; the Society of Architectural Historians of Great Britain (SAHGB) in 1956; and the Society of Architectural Historians, Australia and New Zealand (SAHANZ) in 1985. In 1980, the Vernacular Architecture Forum was founded in the United States to cater for the study of this specialization, as was the International Association for the Study of Traditional Environments, which first met in 1988. Each holds an annual or biannual conference. Since 1988 historians of the modern movement have met biannually at the conferences of the International Working Party for the Documentation and Conservation of the Buildings, Sites and Neighbourhoods of the Modern Movement (Docomomo). Britain's Architectural Humanities Research Association commenced a biannual conference programme in 2004 that places historians of architecture among other disciplinary and interdisciplinary fields. In 2010, the inaugural meeting of the European Architectural History Network will take place in Guimarães, Portugal, building on a number of smaller national and cooperative binational events. Architecture furthermore remains a live subject in many of the world's art history congresses, including the College Art Association, Association of Art Historians, Renaissance Studies Association, Modern Studies Association and the International Congress on Art History, to name a few. These structured, regular meetings are, of course, supplemented each year by hundreds of specialist gatherings at institutes, academies, libraries and universities, or staged independently of all these traditional venues.

5 Among the journals dedicated to the history of architecture are the *Journal of the Society of Architectural Historians* (hereafter *JSAH*, 1941–), *Architectural History* (1956–) and *Fabrications: The Journal of the Society of Architectural Historians, Australia and New Zealand* (1989–). The CISA 'Andrea Palladio' has published a *Bollettino* since 1958, then its *Annali* from 1989. The German journal *Architectura: Zeitschrift für Geschichte der Baukunst* has been in print since 1972. And for decades learned academies and cultural institutes have published proceedings and papers documenting research.

Besides these (merely representative) specialist journals, architecture appears in the pages of interdisciplinary art history,
aesthetics and history journals and cultural studies reviews,
and its history in the pages of journals under the broader classification of the architectural humanities, the vast proliferation
of which we have witnessed since the 1970s.

6 Simona Talenti, *L'histoire de l'architecture en France.
Émergence d'une discipline (1863–1914)* (Paris: Picard, 2000);
David Watkin, *The Rise of Architectural History* (London:
Architectural Press, 1980).

7 Luciano Patetta (ed.), *Storia dell'architettura. Antologia critica*
(Milan: Etas, 1975), 17–54.

8 Demitri Porphyrios (ed.), 'On the Methodology of Architectural
History', special issue, *Architectural Design* 51, nos. 6–7
(1981).

9 Eve Blau (ed.), 'Architectural History 1999/2000', special
issue, *JSAH* 58, no. 3 (September 1999).

10 Zeynep Çelik (ed.), 'Teaching the History of Architecture: A
Global Inquiry', special issues, *JSAH*, Part I, 61, no. 3 (September 2002): 333–96; Part II, 61, no. 4 (December 2002):
509–58; Part III, 62, no. 1 (March 2003): 75–124.

11 For instance, Elisabeth Blair MacDougall (ed.), *The
Architectural Historian in America: A Symposium in
Celebration of the Fiftieth Anniversary of the Founding of the
Society of Architectural Historians*, Studies in the History of
Art 35, Center for Advanced Study in the Visual Arts
Symposium Papers 19 (Washington, DC: National Gallery of
Art; Hanover and London: University Press of New England,
1990); Gwendolyn Wright & Janet Parks (eds.), *The History
of Architecture in American Schools of Architecture, 1865–
1975* (New York: Temple Hoyne Buell Center for the Study
of American Architecture and Princeton Architectural Press,
1990).

12 For example, Andrew Leach, Antony Moulis & Nicole Sully
(eds.), *Shifting Views: Selected Essays in the Architectural
History of Australia and New Zealand* (St Lucia, Qld:
University of Queensland Press, 2008).

13 Anthony Vidler, *Histories of the Immediate Present: Inventing
Architectural Modernism* (Cambridge, Mass.: MIT Press,
2008).

14 Harry Francis Mallgrave, *Modern Architectural Theory: A
Historical Survey, 1673–1968* (Cambridge: Cambridge
University Press, 2005); Hanno-Walter Kruft, *Geschichte
der Architekturtheorie: Von der Antike bis zur Gegenwart*

(Munich: C. H. Beck'she, 1985); Engl. edn, *A History of Architectural Theory from Vitruvius to the Present*, trans. Ronald Taylor, Elsie Callander & Antony Wood (New York: Princeton Architectural Press, 1994).

15 Manfredo Tafuri, *Teorie e storia dell'architettura* (Rome: Laterza, 1968); Engl. edn, *Theories and History of Architecture*, trans. Giorgio Verrecchia from 4th Italian edn (London: Granada, 1980).

16 Compare Ian Hunter, 'The History of Theory', *Critical Inquiry* 33, no. 1 (Autumn 2006): 78–112.

17 K. Michael Hays, 'Notes on Narrative Method in Historical Interpretation', *Footprint* 1 (Autumn 2007): 23–30, 23.

1 Foundations of a modern discipline

1 Compare John Macarthur, 'Some Thoughts on the Canon and Exemplification in Architecture', *Form/Work: An Interdisciplinary Journal of Design and the Built Environment* 5 (2000): 33–45.

2 Nikolaus Pevsner, *An Outline of European Architecture*, 2nd edn ([1943], Harmondsworth: Penguin, 1951), 19.

3 Vitruvius, *The Ten Books on Architecture*, trans. Morris Hicky Morgan ([1914], New York: Dover, 1960), 13.

4 Vitruvius, *Ten Books*, 7.

5 Vitruvius, *Ten Books*, 4.

6 Vitruvius, *Ten Books*, 104.

7 Joseph Rykwert, 'Introduction', *On the Art of Building*, by Leon Battista Alberti ([*De re aedificatoria*, Rome, 1452]; Cambridge, Mass.: MIT Press, 1988), x.

8 Alberti, *On the Art of Building*, 7.

9 Nikolaus Pevsner, 'The Term "Architect" in the Middle Ages', *Speculum* 17, no. 4 (October 1942): 549–62.

10 Giorgio Vasari, *The Lives of the Artists*, trans. Julia Conaway Bondanella and Peter Bondanella ([1550, rev. 1568], Oxford and New York: Oxford University Press, 1991).

11 Walter Benjamin, 'Das Kunstwerk im Zeitalter seiner technischen Reproduzierbarkeit', first published as 'L'œuvre d'art à l'époque de sa reproduction mécanisée', *Zeitschrift für Sozialforschung* [French edn] 5, no. 1 (1936): 40–68; Engl. edn, 'The Work of Art in the Age of Mechanical Reproduction', in *Illuminations: Essays and Reflections*, ed. Hannah Arendt (New York: Pimlico, 1969), 211–44. Carlo Ginzburg, 'Spie. Radici di un paradigma indiriziaio', in *Crisi della ragione*, ed.

Aldo Gargani (Turin: Einaudi, 1979), 57–106; Engl. edn, 'Morelli, Freud and Sherlock Holmes: Clues and Scientific Method', trans. Anna Davin, *History Workshop Journal* 9 (1980): 5–36.

12 Published in English as *The Lives of the Modern Painters, Sculptors, and Architects*, trans. Alice Sedgwick Wohl & Hellmut Wohl ([1672], Cambridge and New York: Cambridge University Press, 2005).

13 Alfred Leroy, *La Vie familière et anecdotique des artistes français du moyen-âge à nos jours* (Paris: Gallimard, 1941).

14 Ernst Kris & Otto Kurz, *Die Legende vom Künstler: Ein historischer Versuch* (Vienna: Krystall, 1934); Engl. edn, *Legend, Myth and Magic in the Image of the Artist: An Historical Experiment*, trans. Alistair Laing with Lottie M. Newman (New Haven, Conn.: Yale University Press, 1979). Kris and Kurz studied with the influential Vienna School Professor, Julius von Schlosser, who also taught the art and architectural historians Ernst Gombrich, Otto Pächt, Fritz Saxl and Hans Sedlmayr.

15 See Lionel Devlieger, 'Benedetto Varchi on the Birth of Artefacts: Architecture, Alchemy and Power in Late-Renaissance Florence', Ph.D. dissertation, Ghent University, 2005.

16 Kris & Kurz, *Legend, Myth and Magic*, 93.

17 Compare Guido Beltramini and Howard Burns (eds.), *L'Architetto. Ruolo, volto, mito* (Venice: Marsilio, 2009).

18 Heinrich Wölfflin, *Kunstgeschichtliche Grundbegriffe. Das Problem der Stilentwicklung in der neueren Kunst* (Munich: Bruckmann, 1915); Engl. edn, *Principles of Art History: The Problem of Development of Style in Later Art*, trans. M. Hottinger from 7th German edn (New York: Dover, 1950). The phrase 'Kunstgeschichte ohne Namen' appears only in the first edition.

19 Compare Benedetto Croce, 'History and Chronicle', in *History: Its Theory and Practice*, trans. Douglas Ainslie ([1911–12], New York: Russell & Russell, 1960), 22.

20 Stanislao Fraschetti, *Il Bernini. La sua vita, la sua opera, il suo tempo* (Milan: Hoepli, 1900); see also Sarah McPhee, 'Costanza Bonarelli: Biography versus Archive', in *Bernini's Biographies: Critical Essays*, ed. Maarten Delbeke, Evonne Levy & Steven Ostrow (University Park: Pennsylvania State University Press, 2007), 315–76.

21 See Louis Callebat (ed.), *Histoire de l'architecte* (Paris: Flammarion, 1998); Andrew Saint, *Architect and Engineer: A Study in Sibling Rivalry* (New Haven, Conn.: Yale University

Press, 2008); Spiro Kostof (ed.), *The Architect: Chapters in the History of the Profession* (Oxford and New York: Oxford University Press, 1977). Thanks to Bart Verschaffel for drawing these studies to my attention.

22 Hubertus Gunther, *Das Studium der antiken Architektur in den Zeichnungen der Hochrenaissance* (Tübingen: Ernst Wasmuth Verlag, 1988).

23 Antonio di Duccio Manetti, *The Life of Brunelleschi*, ed. Howard Saalman, trans. Catherine Enggass (University Park: Pennsylvania State University Press, 1970), 50–5.

24 Branko Mitrovic, 'Andrea Palladio and the Writing of Architectural History', *History as Practice: 25th Annual Conference of the Society of Architectural Historians, Australia and New Zealand*, ed. Ursula de Jong & David Beynon (Geelong, Vic.: SAHANZ, 2008), cd-rom, 2–3.

25 For Pirro's *Anteiquae Urbis Imago*, consult the rich resource 'Illustrated Catalogue of the Maps of Rome Online' at http://db.biblhertz.it/cipro/ (accessed 24 August, 2009). Compare Lola Kantor-Kazovsky, *Piranesi as Interpreter of Roman Architecture and the Origins of his Intellectual World* (Florence: Leo S. Olschki Editore, 2006).

26 Claude Perrault, *Ordonnances des cinq espèces de colonnes selon la méthode des anciens* (Paris: Coignard, 1683); Engl. edn, *Ordonnances for the Five Kinds of Columns after the Method of the Ancients*, trans. Indra Kagis McEwen (Santa Monica, Calif.: Getty Center for the History of Art and Humanities, 1993).

27 Julien-David Le Roy, *Les Ruines des plus beaux monuments de la Grèce. Ouvrage divisé en deux parties, où l'on considère, dans la première, ces monuments du côté de l'histoire; et dans la seconde, du côté de l'architecture* (Paris: Chez H. L. Guerin & L. F. Delatour, 1758); Engl. edn, *The Ruins of the Most Beautiful Monuments of Greece*, trans. David Britt (Los Angeles: Getty Research Institute, 2004); James Stuart & Nicholas Revett, *The Antiquities of Athens* ([1762–1816, 1830], New York: Princeton Architectural Press, 2008).

28 Johann Joachim Winckelmann, *Gedanken über die Nachahmung der Griechischen Werke in der Malerei und Bildhauerkunst* ([Rome, 1755], Ditzingen: Reclam, 1986); Engl. edn, 'On the Imitation of the Painting and Sculpture of the Greeks', in *Writings on Art*, ed. David Irwin (London: Phaidon, 1972), 61–85.

29 Lola Kantor-Kazovsky, 'Pierre Jean Mariette and Piranesi: The Controversy Reconsidered', in *The Serpent and the Stylus:*

Essays on G. B. Piranesi, ed. Mario Bevilacqua, Heather Hyde Minor & Fabio Barry (Ann Arbor, Mich.: University of Michigan Press, 2006), 150. Kantor-Kazovsky points readers to Krzysztof Pomian, 'Mariette et Winckelmann', *Revue Germanique Internationale* 13 (2000): 11–38.

30 Kantor-Kazovsky, *Piranesi*, ch. 1, 'The Graeco-Roman Controversy: Piranesi between Humanism and Enlightenment', 19–58. Piranesi's *Parere* is published in English as *Observations on the Letter of Monsieur Mariette, with Opinions on Architecture, and a Preface to a New Treatise on the Introduction and Progress of the Fine Arts in Europe in Ancient Times*, ed. Caroline Beamish & David Britt (Los Angeles: Getty Research Institute, 2002).

31 Livy, *Ab urbe condita*; Engl. edn, *The History of Rome*, 4 vols. (London: Bell, 1880–1911). Kantor-Kazovsky, *Piranesi*, 50.

32 Michel Foucault, *L'Archéologie du savoir* (Paris: Gallimard, 1970); Engl. edn, *The Archaeology of Knowledge*, trans. A. M. Sheridan Smith (New York: Pantheon, 1972). Foucault's point is beyond the scope of this book, but his thought has proven important to architectural historians in recent decades. Consider Paul Hirst, *Space and Power: Politics, War and Architecture* (Cambridge: Polity, 2005).

33 This analogy is Wölfflin's. See his essay 'Prolegomena to a Psychology of Architecture', in *Empathy, Form and Space: Problems in German Aesthetics, 1873–1893*, trans. & ed. Harry Francis Mallgrave & Eleftherios Ikonomou (Santa Monica: Getty Center for the History of Arts and Humanities, 1994), 149–90, 183. Also Frederic J. Schwartz, 'Cathedrals and Shoes: Concepts of Style in Wölfflin and Adorno', *New German Critique* 76 (Winter 1999): 3–48.

34 See, for example, Joanna Besley, 'Home Improvement, the Popular and the Everyday', in *In the Making: Architecture's Past, 18th Annual Conference of the Society of Architectural Historians, Australia and New Zealand*, ed. Kevin Green (Darwin: SAHANZ, 2001), 305–12; Andrea Renner, 'A Nation that Bathes Together: New York City's Progressive Era Public Baths', and Marta Gutman, 'Race, Place and Play: Robert Moses and the WPA Swimming Pools in New York City', *JSAH* 67, no. 4 (December 2008): 504–31 and 532–61, respectively.

35 On the history and theory of cultural history, I defer to Peter Burke, *What is Cultural History?* (Cambridge: Polity, 2004); and his *Varieties of Cultural History* (Ithaca and London: Cornell University Press, 1997).

36 Jacob Burckhardt, *The Architecture of the Italian Renaissance*, trans. James Palmes ([1867], London: Secker & Warburg; Chicago: University of Chicago Press, 1985), 3.

37 Burckhardt, *The Architecture of the Italian Renaissance*, 3–5, 3.

38 Jules Michelet, *Histoire de France*, vol. VII, *La Renaisance* [1855], rev. edn (Paris: Lacroix, 1986), 10, 6.

39 Jacob Burckhardt, *Die Kultur der Renaissance in Italien* (Basel: Verlag der Schweighauser'schen Verlagsbuchhandlung, 1860); Engl. edn, *The Civilisation of the Renaissance in Italy*, trans. S. G. C. Middlemore (London: George Allen & Unwin, 1937).

40 Compare Paul Oskar Kristeller, *On Renaissance Thought and the Arts: Collected Essays* (Princeton, NJ: Princeton University Press, 1980).

41 Jacob Burckhardt, 'The Qualifications of the Nineteenth Century for the Study of History' [1868–9], in *Reflections on History*, trans. M. D. H. (London: George Allen & Unwin, 1943), 24.

42 Burckhardt, 'The Qualifications of the Nineteenth Century for the Study of History', 31.

43 Charles Darwin, *On the Origin of Species by Means of Natural Selection, or the Preservation of Favoured Races in the Struggle for Life* (London: John Murray, 1859); Gottfried Semper, *Der Stil in den technischen Künsten; oder, Praktische Aesthetik: Ein Handbuch für Techniker, Künstler und Kunstfreunde*, 2 vols. (Frankfurt am Main: Verlag für Kunst & Wissenschaft, 1860); Engl. edn, *Style in the Technical and Tectonic Arts; or, Practical Aesthetics*, trans. Harry Francis Mallgrave & Michael Robinson (Los Angeles: Getty Research Institute, 2004).

44 The relationship between nature and architecture was subject to sustained, culturally mediated debate in the nineteenth century. See, for example, Léonce Reynaud, *Traite d'architecture* (Paris: Carlian-Goery & Dalmont, 1858); and Paula Young Lee's analysis: 'The Meaning of Molluscs: Léonce Reynaud and the Cuvier–Geoffroy Debate of 1830, Paris', *Journal of Architecture* 3, no. 3 (Autumn 1998): 211–40. Consider, too, Barry Bergdoll's authoritative and nuanced synopsis of technological, conceptual and cultural developments in nineteenth-century architecture: *European Architecture 1750–1890*, Oxford History of Art (Oxford and New York: Oxford University Press, 2000).

45 Compare the views of Claude Henri de Saint-Simon (1760–1825) and his disciples, the Saint-Simonists, as summarized in Robin Middleton, 'The Rational Interpretations of Classicism

of Léonce Reynaud and Viollet-le-Duc', *AA Files* 11 (Spring 1986): 29–48, esp. 33, 36.

46 Burckhardt, 'The Qualifications of the Nineteenth Century for the Study of History', 28.

47 Wölfflin, 'Prolegomena', 182.

48 Alois Riegl, *Stilfragen. Grundlegungen zu einer Geschichte der Ornamentik* (Berlin: Siemens, 1893), and *Die spätrömische Kunstindustrie nach den Funden in Österreich-Ungarn* (Vienna: Kaiserlich-Königliche Hof- und Staatsdruckerei, 1901).

49 Christopher S. Wood (ed.), *The Vienna School Reader: Politics and Art Historical Method in the 1930s* (New York: Zone Books, 2000), 22–43.

50 Most notably in Cornelius Gurlitt, *Geschichte des Barockstiles in Italien* (Stuttgart: Ebner and Seubert, 1887), and *Geschichte des Barockstiles, des Rococo, und des Klassicismus in Belgien, Holland, Frankreich, England* (Stuttgart: Ebner & Seubert, 1888).

51 August Schmarsow, *Barock und Rokoko: Das Malerische in der Architektur: Eine kritische Auseinandersetzung* (Leipzig: S. Hirzel, 1897).

52 See Mark Jarzombek, *The Psychologizing of Modernity: Art, Architecture and History* (Cambridge: Cambridge University Press, 1999), ch. 1; Mallgrave & Ikonomou (eds.), *Empathy, Form, and Space.*

53 Watkin, *The Rise of Architectural History*, esp. 1–10, 20–9, 30–2; compare Anthony Grafton, *What Was History? The Art of History in Early Modern Europe* (Cambridge: Cambridge University Press, 2007).

54 Joseph Gwilt, *An Encyclopædia of Architecture*, rev. edn ([1842], London: Longmans, Green & Co., 1881); James Fergusson, *An Historical Inquiry into the True Principles of Beauty in Art, Especially with Reference to Architecture* (London: Longman, 1849), and *History of Indian and Eastern Architecture* (London: Murray, 1899); Banister Fletcher, *A History of Architecture for the Student, Craftsman, and Amateur, Being a Comparative View of the Historical Styles from the Earliest Period* (London: T. Batsford, 1896).

55 On the 'French' (as opposed to German) sense of *archéologie*, compare Julius von Schlosser, 'The Vienna School of the History of Art: Review of a Century of Austrian Scholarship in German' [1934], trans. & ed. Karl Johns, *Journal of Art Historiography* 1 (December 2009, 6, online at www.gla.ac.uk/departments/arthistoriography (accessed 7 January 2010).

56 Elisabeth Blair MacDougall, 'Before 1870: Founding Fathers and Amateur Historians', and William B. Rhoades, 'The Discovery of America's Architectural Past, 1874–1914)', in *The Architectural Historian in America*, 15–20 & 23–39, respectively.

57 Henri Focillon, *La Vie des formes* (Paris: Presses Universitaires de France, 1934); Engl. edn, *The Life of Forms in Art*, trans. Charles B. Hogan & George Kubler ([1948], New York: Zone Books, 1989).

58 Louis Hautecœur, *Histoire de l'architecture classique en France*, 7 vols. (Paris: Picard, 1948–57).

59 Wilhelm Worringer, 'Abstraktion und Einfühlung. Ein Beitrag zur Stilpsychologie', doctoral dissertation, Universität Bern, 1907. Published 1908 (Munich: Piper). See also Worringer's *Schriften*, 2 vols., ed. Hannes Böhringer & Helga Grebing (Munich: Fink, 2004).

2 Organizing the past

1 Johann Gottfried Herder, *Reflections on the Philosophy of the History of Mankind*, trans. Frank E. Manual ([1784–91, 4 vols.] Chicago and London: University of Chicago Press, 1968), esp. 79, in 'Humanity the End of Human Nature'. Compare Peter Kohane, 'Interpreting Past and Present: An Approach to Architectural History', *Architectural Theory Review* 2, no. 1 (1997): 30–7.

2 Carl Albert Rosenthal, 'In What Style Should We Build?' in *In What Style Should We Build?* by Heinrich Hübsch, Rudolf Wiegmann, Carl Albert Rosenthal et al., trans. & ed. David Britt ([1829] Los Angeles: Getty Center for the History of Art and the Humanities, 1992), 114.

3 George Selwyn, 'Parish Churches in New Zealand', *Ecclesiologist* (1841), cited in Robin Skinner, 'Representations of Architecture and New Zealand in London, 1841–1860', Ph.D. dissertation, University of Auckland, 2007, 163–224, 168.

4 As a symptom, see Jean Étienne Casimir Barberot, *Histoire des styles d'architecture dans tous les pays, depuis les temps anciens jusqu'à nos jours*, 2 vols. (Paris: Baudrey et cie, 1891).

5 For a longer list of additional anthologies, monographs and themed issues of journals concerned with approaches to architectural historiography, see the 'Further reading' section.

6   Mark Roskill, *What is Art History?* 2nd edn ([1976], London: Thames and Hudson, 1989).

7   W. Eugene Kleinbauer and Thomas P. Slavens, *Research Guide to the History of Western Art* (Chicago: American Library Association, 1982).

8   Laurie Schneider Adams, *The Methodologies of Art* (Boulder, Colo.: Westview Press, 1996).

9   Michael Podro, *The Critical Historians of Art* (New Haven & London: Yale University Press, 1982).

10   Otto Pächt, *Methodisches zur kunsthistorischen Praxis*, ed. Jorg Oberhaidacher, Arthur Rosenauer & Gertraut Schikola (Munich: Prestel, 1986); Engl. edn, *The Practice of Art History: Reflections on Method*, trans. David Britt (London: Harvey Miller, 1999).

11   James S. Ackerman, 'Style', in *Distance Points: Essays in Theory and Renaissance Art and Culture* (Cambridge, Mass.: MIT Press, 1991), rev. from 'A Theory of Style', *Journal of Aesthetics and Art Criticism* 20, no. 3 (1962): 227–37.

12   Ackerman, 'Style', 3.

13   Ackerman, 'Style', 3–4.

14   Ackerman, 'Style', 4. Artistic style has been subject to much theorization. See, for example, Beryl Lang, *The Concept of Style*, rev. edn ([1979], Ithaca & London: Cornell University Press, 1987); Caroline van Eck, James McAllister & Renée van de Vall (eds.), *The Question of Style in Philosophy and the Arts* (Cambridge: Cambridge University Press, 1995); Andrew Benjamin, *Style and Time* (Chicago: Northwestern University Press, 2006).

15   Compare David Summers, 'Art History Reviewed II: Heinrich Wölfflin's "Kunstgeschichtliche Grundbegriffe", 1915', *Burlington Magazine* 151, no. 1276 (July 2009): 476–9.

16   Peter Gay, *Style in History* (New York: Basic Books, 1974), 7.

17   Ackerman, 'Style', 4.

18   Ackerman, 'Style', 4–5.

19   Émile Bayard, *L'Art de reconnaître les styles* (Paris: Librairie Garnier Frères, 1900).

20   François Benoit, *L'Architecture*, Manuels d'histoire de l'arte, 4 vols. (Paris: Laurens, 1911).

21   On this problem, see Mark Crinson & Claire Zimmerman (eds.), *Neo-avant-garde to Postmodern: Postwar Architecture in Britain and Beyond*, Yale Studies in British Art 21 (New Haven, Conn.: Yale University Press, 2010).

22   Ethan Matt Kavaler, 'Renaissance Gothic: Pictures of Geometry and Narratives of Ornament', *Art History* 29 (2006): 1–46. A

conference at the Institut national d'histoire de l'art (Paris, 12–16 June 2007) considered this pairing in some detail under the title 'Le Gothique de la Renaissance'.

23 This point draws on comments made to me by John Macarthur, who has served in this capacity. Compare Paul Walker & Stuart King, 'Style and Climate in Addison's Brisbane Exhibition Building', *Fabrications* 17, no. 2 (December 2007): 22–43, esp. 23–8.

24 Arnold Hauser, *Social History of Art*, 4 vols. ([1951–], London: Routledge & Kegan Paul, 1962); and *Philosophy of Art History* (London: Routledge; New York: Knopf, 1959), esp. 'Wölfflin and Historicism', 119–39.

25 See, for example, Charles Burroughs, *From Signs to Design: Environmental Process and Reform in Early Renaissance Rome* (Cambridge, Mass.: MIT Press, 1990); Manfredo Tafuri, *Venezia e il rinascimento. Religione, scienza, architettura* (Turin: Einaudi, 1985); Engl. edn, *Venice and the Renaissance*, trans. Jessica Levine (Cambridge, Mass.: MIT Press, 1995) – compare Tafuri, *Humanism, Technical Knowledge and Rhetoric: The Debate in Renaissance Venice* (Cambridge, Mass.: Harvard Graduate School of Design, 1986); Deborah Howard, *Venice and the East: The Impact of the Islamic World on Venetian Architecture, 1100–1500* (New Haven, Conn.: Yale University Press, 2000).

26 Hessel Miedema, 'On Mannerism and *maniera*', *Simiolus: Netherlands Quarterly for the History of Art* 10, no. 1 (1978–9): 19–45. Compare the panel dedicated to this theme and chaired by Ernst Gombrich, 'Recent Concepts of Mannerism', in *Studies in Western Art: Acts of the Twentieth International Conference of the History of Art*, vol. II, *The Renaissance and Mannerism*, ed. Ida E. Rubin (Princeton, NJ: Princeton University Press, 1963), 163–255. This included contributions by Craig Hugh Smyth, John Shearman, Frederick Hartt and Wolfgang Lodz. Franklin W. Robinson & Stephen G. Nichols, Jr (eds.), *The Meaning of Mannerism* (Hannover, NH: University Press of New England, 1972). Compare Craig Hugh Smyth, *Mannerism and Maniera* (Locust Valley, NY: J. J. Augustin, 1962) and John Shearman, *Mannerism* (Harmondsworth: Penguin, 1967).

27 Antonio di Tuccio Manetti, *The Life of Brunelleschi*, ed. Howard Saalman, trans. Catherine Enggass (University Park: Pennsylvania State University Press, 1970).

28 Compare Focillon's observation in *La vie des formes* that the division of historical time by century lends the century itself a biographical character.

29   Terrence Riley & Barry Bergdoll (eds.), *Mies in Berlin* (New York: Museum of Modern Art, 2001); Phyllis Lambert (ed.), *Mies in America* (New York: Harry S. Abrams, 2001).

30   Marco De Michelis, *Heinrich Tessenow, 1876–1950* (Milan: Electa, 1993); Claude Laurens, *Architecture. Projets et réalisations de 1934 à 1971*, ed. Johan Lagae, Vlees en Beton 53–4 (Ghent: Vakgroep Architectuur en Stedenbouw, Universiteit Gent, 2001).

31   One recent book that attends to this complexity from the perspective of a New Zealand case is Justine Clark & Paul Walker, *Looking for the Local: Architecture and the New Zealand Modern* (Wellington: Victoria University Press, 2000). For Clark and Walker, New Zealand architects operate between processes of reception and invention, and the idea of the local enters a relationship with the anti-local.

32   Compare Thomas DaCosta Kaufmann, *Toward a Geography of Art* (Chicago: University of Chicago Press, 2004).

33   G. E. Kidder Smith, *Switzerland Builds: Its Native and Modern Architecture* (London: Architectural Press; New York & Stockholm: Albert Bonnier, 1950), 21. See also Giedion's introductory essay, 'Switzerland or the Forming of an Idea', 11–17.

34   Jul Bachmann & Stanislaus von Moos, *New Directions in Swiss Architecture* (London: Studio Vista, 1969), 11.

35   Eberhard Hempel, *Baroque Art and Architecture in Central Europe: Germany, Austria, Switzerland, Hungary, Czechoslovakia, Poland. Painting and Sculpture: Seventeenth and Eighteenth Centuries; Architecture: Sixteenth to Eighteenth Centuries*, trans. Elizabeth Hempel & Marguerite Kay (Harmondsworth: Pelican, 1965).

36   Antoine Quatremère de Quincy, 'Type', trans. in Samir Younés, *The True, the Fictive, and the Real: The Historical Dictionary of Architecture of Quatremère de Quincy* (London: Andreas Papadakis, 1999), 254–5. Younés's edition contains selected translations from Quatremère de Quincy, *Dictionnaire historique d'architecture comprenant dans son plan les notions historiques, descriptives, archéologiques, biographiques, théoriques, didactiques et pratiques de cet art*, 2 vols. (Paris: A. Le Clère, 1832).

37   Marc-Antoine Laugier, *Essai sur l'architecture* (Paris: Chez Duchesne, 1753).

38   Anthony Vidler, 'The Third Typology' [1977], in *Architecture Theory since 1968*, ed. K. Michael Hays (Cambridge, Mass.: MIT Press, 1998), 288–93.

39   Vidler, 'The Third Typology', 290.

40   Maarten Delbeke considers the historical and historiographical implications of ecclesiastical architectural histories in 'Architecture and the Genres of History Writing in Ecclesiastical Historiography', in *Limits disciplinaires. Repenser les limites. L'Architecture a travers l'espace, le temps et les disciplines* (2005), available online at www.inha.fr/colloques/document. php?id=1800 (accessed 15 October 2009).

41   Daniel Sherer, 'Typology and its Vicissitudes: Observations on a Critical Category', *Précis* 33 (1997): 41–6. Compare Pier Vittorio Aureli, 'The Difficult Whole: Typology and the Singularity of the Urban Event in Aldo Rossi's Early Theoretical Work, 1953–1964', *Log* 9 (Winter–Spring 2007): 39–61. On the status of architectural typology in architectural design and historiography respectively, see Giulio Carlo Argan's essay 'Sul concetto di tipologia architettonica' (1962), published as 'On the Typology of Architecture', trans. Joseph Rykwert, in *Theorizing a New Agenda for Architecture: An Anthology of Architectural Theory, 1965–1995*, ed. Kate Nesbitt (New York: Princeton Architectural Press, 1996), 242–6.

42   Nikolaus Pevsner, *A History of Building Types* (London: Thames and Hudson, 1976), 9.

43   Pevsner, *A History of Building Types*, 'Foreword'.

44   Carroll L. V. Meeks, *The Railroad Station: An Architectural History* (New Haven, Conn.: Yale University Press, 1956); Johan Friedrich Geist, *Passagen, ein Bautyp des 19 Jahrhunderts* (Munich: Prestel, 1969); Engl. edn, *Arcades: The History of a Building Type*, trans. Jane O. Newman (Cambridge, Mass.: MIT Press, 1983). The popularity of Geist's history has more recently been eclipsed by interest in Walter Benjamin's mammoth study on the subject, posthumously named *Das Passagen-Werk*, ed. Rolf Tiedemenn (Frankfurt am Main: Suhrkamp Verlag, 1983); Engl. edn, *The Arcades Project*, trans. Howard Eiland & Kevin McLaughlin (Cambridge, Mass.: Belknap Press, 1999).

45   Pevsner, *A History of Building Types*, 'Foreword'.

46   Pevsner, *A History of Building Types*, 289.

47   Michael Webb, *Architecture in Britain Today* (Feltham: Country Life, 1969).

48   Igea Troiani, 'Deserved Exposure: Stuart McIntosh's Architecture, 1953–63', *Fabrications* 16, no. 2 (December 2006): 28–43.

49   Wouter Davidts, *Bouwen voor de Kunst? Museumarchitectuur van Centre Pompidou tot Tate Modern* (Ghent: A&S Books, 2006).

50 Among the possible counter-examples, two occur to me: Annemarie Adams, *Medicine by Design: The Architect and the Modern Hospital, 1893–1943* (Minneapolis: University of Minnesota Press, 2008); and Joseph Connors, *Borromini and the Roman Oratory: Style and Society* (Cambridge, Mass.: MIT Press; New York: Architectural History Foundation, 1980). Paul Walker also reminded me of the important example provided by Paul Rabinow's *French Modern: Norms and Forms of the Social Environment* (Cambridge, Mass.: MIT Press, 1989).

51 Reyner Banham, 'A Black Box: The Secret Profession of Architecture' [1990], in *A Critic Writes: Essays by Reyner Banham*, selected by Mary Banham, Paul Barker, Sutherland Lyall & Cedric Price (Berkeley & Los Angeles: University of California Press, 1996), 292–9.

52 Contrast, for example, Ronald Lewcock, ' "Generative Concepts" in Vernacular Architecture', in *Vernacular Architecture in the Twenty-First Century*, ed. Lindsay Asquith & Marcel Vellinga (London and New York: Routledge, 2006), 199–214.

53 Sigfried Giedion, *Space, Time, and Architecture: The Growth of a New Tradition* (Cambridge, Mass.: Harvard University Press, 1941).

54 Sigfried Giedion, *The Eternal Present: A Contribution on Constancy and Change*, 2 vols. (New York: Pantheon, 1962).

55 Christian Norberg-Schulz, *Intentions in Architecture* (Cambridge, Mass.: MIT Press, 1965); *Existence, Space, and Architecture* (London: Studio Vista, 1971); *Meaning in Western Architecture* (New York: Praeger, 1975). Compare Jorge Otero-Pailos, 'Photo[historio]graphy: Christian Norberg-Schulz's Demotion of Textual History', *JSAH* 66, no. 2 (June 2007): 220–41.

56 John Macarthur & Antony Moulis, 'Movement and Figurality: The Circulation Diagram and the History of the Architectural Plan', in *Celebration: 22nd Annual Conference of the Society of Architectural Historians, Australia and New Zealand*, ed. Andrew Leach & Gill Matthewson (Napier, NZ: SAHANZ, 2005), 231.

57 Macarthur & Moulis, 'Movement and Figurality', 231.

58 Published in the *Opera varie di architettura, prospettive, grotteschi, antichità*, reproduced in *Giovanni Battista Piranesi: The Complete Etchings*, vol. I, ed. John Wilton Ely (San Francisco: Alan Wofsy Fine Arts, 1994), 82.

59   Colin Rowe, 'The Mathematics of the Ideal Villa', *Architectural Review* (March 1947): 101–4; and in Rowe, *The Mathematics of the Ideal Villa and Other Essays* (Cambridge, Mass.: MIT Press, 1982), 1–28.

60   Manfredo Tafuri, *Progetto e utopia. Architettura e sviluppo capitalistico* (Bari: Laterza, 1973); Engl. edn, *Architecture and Utopia: Design and Capitalist Development*, trans. Barbara Luigi la Penta (Cambridge, Mass.: MIT Press, 1976).

61   For a full list of Tafuri's writing, see the bibliography in Andrew Leach, *Manfredo Tafuri: Choosing History* (Ghent: A&S Books, 2007), 287–322.

62   Compare Jean-Louis Cohen's observations on architectural history and politics in his 'Field Note', 'Scholarship or Politics? Architectural History and the Risks of Autonomy', *JSAH* 67, no. 3 (September 2008): 325–9.

63   William J. Mitchell, *City of Bits: Space, Place, and the Infobahn* (Cambridge, Mass.: MIT Press, 1995), 8.

64   Jean-François Lyotard, *Moralités postmodernes* (Paris: Éditions Galilée, 1993); Engl. edn, *Postmodern Fables*, trans. Georges van den Abbeele (Minneapolis: University of Minnesota Press, 1997); Douglas Coupland, *Microserfs* (New York: HarperCollins, 1995).

65   Beatriz Colomina (ed.), *Sexuality and Space* (New York: Princeton Architectural Press, 1992); Diana Agrest, Patricia Conway & Leslie Kanes Weisman (eds.), *The Sex of Architecture* (New York: Harry N. Abrams, 1996); Joel Sanders (ed.), *Stud: Architectures of Masculinity* (New York: Princeton Architectural Press, 1996).

3   Evidence

1   A. S. Byatt, *The Biographer's Tale* (New York: Vintage, 2001).

2   Routledge has published an important catalogue of such studies since 1999 in the series 'Architext', which includes, but is not limited to, postcolonial history and theory of architecture.

3   See articles by Karen Beckman, Sarah Williams-Goldhagen, George Dodds, Judi Loach, Nancy Levinson, and Judith Rodenbeck under the title 'On the Line: A Forum of Editors', *JSAH* 68, no. 2 (June 2009): 148–57.

4   See Peter Burke, *The French Historical Revolution: The Annales School 1929–89* (Stanford, Calif.: Stanford University Press, 1990), 42.

5 Matthew A. Cohen, 'How Much Brunelleschi? A Late Medieval Proportional System in the Basilica of San Lorenzo', *JSAH* 67, no. 1 (March 2008): 18–57.

6 Cohen, 'How Much Brunelleschi?' 44–5.

7 Roberta Battaglia, 'A First Collection of the *Vedute di Roma*: Some New Elements on the States', in *The Serpent and the Stylus: Essays on G. B. Piranesi*, ed. Mario Bevilacqua, Heather Hyde Minor & Fabio Barry (Ann Arbor: University of Michigan Press for the American Academy in Rome, 2005), 93–119.

8 Battaglia, 'A First Collection of the *Vedute di Roma*', 99.

9 Antony Moulis, 'Transcribing the Contemporary City: Le Corbusier, Adelaide and Chandigarh', *From Panorama to Paradise: Proceedings of the 24th Annual Conference of the Society of Architectural Historians, Australia and New Zealand*. ed. Stephen Loo & Katharine Bartsch (Adelaide: SAHANZ, 2007), cd-rom.

10 Moulis, 'Transcribing the Contemporary City', 7–8.

11 Moulis, 'Transcribing the Contemporary City', 8–9.

12 Ginzburg, 'Spie'; Engl. edn, 'Morelli, Freud and Sherlock Holmes'. See ch. 1, n. 11.

13 Carlo Ginzburg, *The Judge and the Historian: Marginal Notes on a Late-Twentieth-Century Miscarriage of Justice*, trans. Anthony Shugaar ([1991], London and New York: Verso, 1999), 17.

14 Pieter Martins, 'La destruction de Thérouanne et d'Hesdin par Charles Quint en 1553', in *La forteresse à l'épreuve du temps. Destruction, dissolution, dénaturation, XIe–XXe siècle*, ed. Gilles Blieck, Philippe Contamine, Christian Corvisier & Nicolas Faucherre (Paris: Comité des travaux historiques et scientifiques, 2007), 63–117.

15 Compare Deidre Brown, *Maori Architecture: From Fale to Wharenui and Beyond* (Auckland: Raupo, 2009).

16 Andrew Ballantyne, 'Architecture as Evidence', in *Rethinking Architectural Historiography*, ed. Dana Arnold, Elvan Altan Ergut & Belgin Turan Özkaya (London and New York: Routledge, 2006), 38.

17 Maristella Casciato & Stanislaus von Moos (eds.), *Twilight of the Plan: Chandigarh and Brasília* (Mendrisio: Mendrisio Academy Press, 2007).

18 Stanislaus von Moos, 'Vers une "Grille ChaBra": Notes on the Exhibition', in *Twilight of the Plan*, ed. Casciato & von Moos, 39–40.

19 Nicole Coldstream, 'The Architect, History and Architectural History', *Transactions of the Royal Historical Society* 13 (2003), 220.

4 How useful?

1 Tafuri, 'Theories and History of Architecture', 36–40. Compare Nikolaus Pevsner, *Pioneers of Modern Design: From William Morris to Walter Gropius* ([1936] London: Faber & Faber, 1936).

2 Bruno Zevi & Paolo Portoghesi (eds.), *Michelangiolo architetto* (Turin: Einaudi, 1964), esp. Zevi, 'Introduzione: Attualità di Michelangiolo architetto', 9–27; Tafuri, *Theories and History of Architecture*, 141–70; and Tafuri, *Ricerca del rinascimento. Principi, città, architettura* (Turin: Einaudi, 1992), Engl. edn, *Interpreting the Renaissance: Princes, Cities, Architects*, trans. Daniel Sherer (New Haven, Conn.: Yale University Press, 2006), esp. xxvii–xxix.

3 Gwilt, *An Encyclopædia of Architecture*; Diana Ketcham, *Le Désert de Retz: A Late Eighteenth-Century French Folly Garden, The Artful Landscape of Monsieur de Monville* (Cambridge, Mass.: MIT Press, 1994); Andreas Schönle, *The Ruler in the Garden: Politics and Landscape Design in Imperial Russia* (Oxford and Bern: Peter Lang, 2007).

4 Compare Yves Schoonjans, *Architectuur en Vooruitgang: De Cultuur van het Eclecticisme in de 19de eeuw* (Ghent: A&S Books, 2007).

5 Benedetto Croce, *History: Its Theory and Practice*, trans. Douglas Ainslie (New York: Russell & Russell, 1960). For this discussion, see esp. 'History and Chronicle', 11–26.

6 Jacob Burckhardt, *Judgments on History and Historians*, trans. Harry Zohn ([1958], Indianapolis, Ind.: Liberty Fund, 1999), 168.

7 L. P. Hartley, *The Go-Between* (London: Hamish Hamilton, 1953), 9.

8 Croce, *History*, 22.

9 E. H. Carr, *What is History?* 2nd edn, ed. R. W. Davies ([1961], Harmondsworth: Penguin, 1984), 10–11.

10 Compare Paul Memmott, *Gunyah, Goondie + Wurley: The Aboriginal Architecture of Australia* (St Lucia, Qld: University of Queensland Press, 2007); Elisabeth Pigou-Dennis, 'Fabricating a Space and an Architecture: The Rastafarian

Experience in Jamaica', in *Formulation Fabrications: The Architecture of History, Proceedings of the 17th Annual Conference of the Society of Architectural Historians, Australia and New Zealand* (Wellington: SAHANZ, 2000), 73–83.

11 Carr, *What is History?* 12.

12 Evonne Levy and Jens Baumgarten posed this distinction of a number of scholars around the theme of the baroque, in 'Our Baroque Confection', *Revista canadiense de estudios hispánicos* 33, no. 1 (Autumn 2008): 39–64, esp. 57–61.

13 Henry A. Millon, 'History of Architecture – How Useful?' *AIA Journal* 34, no. 6 (December 1960): 23–5.

14 Millon, 'History of Architecture – How Useful?' 24–5.

15 Millon, 'History of Architecture – How Useful?' 25.

16 Bruno Zevi, Introduction to 'L'opera architettonica di Michelangiolo nel quarto centenario della morte. Modelli, fotografie e commenti degli studenti dell'Istituto di Architettura di Venezia', *Architettura. Cronache e storia* 9, no. 99 (January 1964): 654–712.

17 Millon, 'History of Architecture – How Useful?' 25.

18 Tafuri, *Theories and History of Architecture*, 151, 156.

19 A term advanced in Julie Willis & Philip Goad, 'A Bigger Picture: Reframing Australian Architectural History', *Fabrications* 18, no. 1 (June 2008): 6–23, esp. 16–19.

20 Carr, *What is History?* 23.

5 History and theory

1 Peter Collins, *Changing Ideals in Modern Architecture* (London: Faber & Faber, 1965); Joseph Rykwert, *The First Moderns: The Architects of the Eighteenth Century* (Cambridge, Mass.: MIT Press, 1980); Kenneth Frampton, *Modern Architecture: A Critical History* (London: Thames & Hudson, 1980). Compare Joseph Rykwert, *The Judicious Eye: Architecture against the Other Arts* (Chicago: University of Chicago Press, 2008); and John Macarthur, *The Picturesque: Architecture, Disgust, and Other Irregularities* (London: Routledge, 2007).

2 Jean-François Lyotard, *La condition postmoderne. Rapport sur le savoir* (Paris: Minuit, 1979), Engl. edn, *The Postmodern Condition: A Report on Knowledge*, trans. Geoffrey Bennington and Brian Massumi (Minneapolis: University of Minnesota Press, 1984).

3   Jacques Derrida, *De la grammatologie* (Paris: Minuit, 1967), Engl. edn, *Of Grammatology*, rev. edn, trans. Gayatri Spivak (Baltimore: Johns Hopkins University Press, 1976).

4   Andrew Leach & John Macarthur, 'Tafuri as Theorist', *arq: Architectural Research Quarterly* 10, nos. 3–4 (2006): 235–40.

5   This period of writing has been thoroughly anthologized: Joan Ockman (ed.), *Architectural Culture, 1943–1968: A Documentary Anthology* (New York: Rizzoli, 1993); Kate Nesbitt (ed.), *Theorizing a New Agenda for Architecture An Anthology of Architectural Theory, 1965–1995* (New York: Princeton Architectural Press, 1996); K. Michael Hays (ed.), *The Oppositions Reader* (Cambridge, Mass.: MIT Press, 1998), and (ed.), *Architecture Theory since 1968* (Cambridge, Mass.: MIT Press, 1998); Hilde Heynen, André Loeckx, Lieven De Cauter & Karina van Herck (eds.), *'Dat is architectuur': Sleutelteksten uit de Twintigste Eeuw* (Rotterdam: 010, 2001).

6   Vidler, *Histories of the Immediate Present*, 3.

7   Sokratis Georgiadis, *Sigfried Giedion: Eine Intellektuelle Biographie* (Zurich: Amman, 1989), Engl. edn, *Sigfried Giedion: An Intellectual Biography*, trans. Colin Hall (Edinburgh: Edinburgh University Press, 1993).

8   Hunter, 'The History of Theory', 80.

9   Iain Borden, 'What is Architectural History and Theory?' in *Bartlett Book of Ideas*, ed. Peter Cook (London: Bartlett Books of Architecture, 2000), 8.

10   Terry Eagleton, *After Theory* (London: Basic Books, 2003), cited in Hunter, 'The History of Theory', 86.

11   Christoph L. Frommel, *The Architecture of the Italian Renaissance* (London: Thames and Hudson, 2007).

12   Hunter, 'The History of Theory', 81.

13   Hunter, 'The History of Theory', 80.

14   Discussed by Henry A. Millon and Stanford Anderson in keynote addresses to 'Geschichte und Theorie im Architekturunterricht', Bibliothek Werner Oechslin, Einsiedeln, 20–22 November 2009.

15   Jean-Louis Cohen, 'La coupure entre architectes et intellectuels, ou les enseignements de l'italophilie', *Extenso* 1 (1984): 182–223.

16   Beatriz Colomina in a paper presented at the conference on 'The Critical Legacies of Manfredo Tafuri', Columbia University and the Cooper Union, New York, 21 April 2006.

17   For a later, British response to this phenomenon, compare the Routledge series Thinkers for Architects, which considers a number of philosophers and their relevance to architecture:

Luce Irigaray (Peg Rawes, 2007), Martin Heidegger (Adam Sharr, 2007), Gilles Deleuze and Felix Guattari (Andrew Ballantyne, 2007), Maurice Merleau-Ponty (Jonathan Hale, 2009) and Homi Bhabha (Felipe Hernandez, 2009). An older example, tracking the reading programme of the University of Nottingham's MA in Architecture and Critical Theory, is Neil Leach (ed.), *Rethinking Architecture: A Reader in Cultural Theory* (London and New York: Routledge, 1997).

18 www.institute-ny.org (accessed 9 April 2009).

19 The series Oppositions Books, published by MIT Press, included Alan Colquhoun, *Essays in Architectural Criticism: Modern Architecture and Historical Change* (1981); Moisei Ginzburg, *Style and Epoch*, trans. Anatole Senkevich (1982); Adolf Loos, *Spoken into the Void: Collected Essays, 1897–1900*, trans. Jane O. Newman & John H. Smith (1982); Aldo Rossi, *Architecture of the City*, trans. Diane Ghirardo & Joan Ockman (1982); and *Scientific Autobiography*, trans. Lawrence Venuti (1982).

20 Teresa Stoppani, 'Unfinished Business: The Critical Project after Manfredo Tafuri', in *Critical Architecture*, ed. Jane Rendell, Jonathan Hill, Murray Fraser & Mark Dorrian (London and New York: Routledge, 2007), 22–30.

21 Jennifer Bloomer, *Architecture and the Text: The (S)crypts of Joyce and Piranesi* (New Haven, Conn.: Yale University Press, 1993).

22 www.gsd.harvard.edu/research/publications/affiliated_publications/assemblage/assemb41.html (accessed 15 April 2009).

23 K. Michael Hays, 'Notes on Narrative Method in Historical Interpretation', *Footprint* (Autumn 2007): 23.

24 Reinhold Martin, *The Organizational Complex: Architecture, Media, and Corporate Space* (Cambridge, Mass.: MIT Press, 2005); Felicity D. Scott, *Architecture or Techno-utopia: Politics after Modernism* (Cambridge, Mass.: MIT Press, 2007).

25 Compare Wood (ed.), *The Vienna School Reader*. Evonne Levy is pursuing this theme into the specific field of baroque historiography with her book project 'Barock: Architectural History and Politics from Burckhardt to Hitler (1844–1945)'. See www.nga.gov/casva/fellowships.html.

26 www.anycorp.com/log/ (accessed 15 April 2009); see also Atelier Bow-Wow, *Walking with Atelier Bow-Wow: Kanazawa Machiya Metabolism*, 21st Century Museum of Contemporary Art, Kanazawa, 2007, project archive at www.bow-wow.jp/profile/publications_e.html (accessed 15 April 2009).

27 See the Routledge book series Architext, edited by Thomas A. Markus and Anthony D. King.

28 'Think-tank: Counter-theses after 9.11.01' at www.arch. columbia.edu/index.php?pageData=2937 (accessed 15 April 2009).

29 'Aggregate: Working Conference' http://artlibrary.wordpress. com/2008/04/08/75/ (accessed 15 April 2009).

30 Eyal Weizman, *Hollow Land: Israel's Architecture of Occupation* (London: Verso, 2007).

31 Hays, 'Notes on Narrative Method in Historical Interpretation', 29.

Further reading

Ackerman, James. 'On American Scholarship in the Arts'. *College Art Journal* 17, no. 4 (Summer 1958): 357–62.
——— 'The 50 Years of CISA'. *Annali di Architettura* 20 (2008): 9–11.
Agosti, Giacomo. *La nascita della storia dell'arte in Italia: Adolfo Venturi dal museo all'università, 1880–1940*. Venice: Marsolio, 1996.
Allsopp, Bruce. *The Study of Architectural History*. New York: Praeger, 1970.
Amery, Colin. 'Art History Reviewed IV: Nikolaus Pevsner's "Pioneers of the Modern Movement", 1936'. *Burlington Magazine* 151, no. 1278 (September 2009): 617–19.
Arnold, Dana (ed.). *Reading Architectural History*. London and New York: Routledge, 2002.
Arnold, Dana, Elvan Altan Ergut & Belgin Turan Özkaya (eds.). *Rethinking Architectural Historiography*. London and New York: Routledge, 2006.
Attoe, Wayne, & Charles W. Moore (eds.). 'How Not to Teach Architectural History'. Special issue, *Journal of Architectural Education [JAE]* 34, no. 1 (Fall 1980).
Bardati, Flaminia (ed.). *Storia dell'arte e storia dell'architettura. Un dialogo difficile*. San Casciano: Libro Co., 2007.
Bazin, Germain. *Histoire de l'histoire de l'art. De Vasari à nos jours*. Paris: Albin Michel, 1986.
Binfield, Clyde (ed.). 'Architecture and History: A Joint Symposium of the Royal Historical Society and the Society of Architectural Historians of Great Britain, Held at Tapton Hall, University of

Sheffield, 5–7 April 2002'. Papers presented in *Transactions of the Royal Historical Society* 13 (December 2003): 187–392.

Biraghi, Marco. *Progetto di crisi. Manfredo Tafuri e l'architettura contemporanea.* Milan: Christian Marinotti, 2005.

Blau, Eve. 'Plenary Address, Society of Architectural Historians Annual Meeting, Richmond, Virginia, 18 April 2002: A Question of Discipline'. *JSAH* 62, no. 1 (March 2003): 125–9.

—— (ed.). 'Architectural History 1999/2000'. Special issue, *Journal of the Society of Architectural Historians [JSAH]* 58, no. 3 (September 1999).

Borden, Iain. 'What is Architectural History and Theory?' In *Bartlett Book of Ideas*, ed. Peter Cook, 68–70. London: Bartlett Books of Architecture, 2000.

Borden, Iain, & Jane Rendell (eds.). *Intersections: Architectural Histories and Critical Theories.* London and New York: Routledge, 2000.

Böröcz, Zsuzsanna & Luc Verpoest (eds.). *Imag(in)ing Architecture: Iconography in Nineteenth-Century Architectural Historical Publications.* Leuven and Voorburg: Acco, 2008.

Briggs, Martin. *The Architect in History.* Oxford: Clarendon Press, 1927.

Brown, Deidre, & Andrew Leach (eds.). 'A Regional Practice'. Special issue, *Fabrications: The Journal of the Society of Architectural Historians, Australia and New Zealand* 17, no. 2 (2008).

Brucculeri, Antonio. *Louis Hautecœur et l'architecture classique en France. Du dessein historique à l'action publique.* Paris: Picard, 2007.

Çelik, Zeynep (ed.). 'Teaching the History of Architecture: A Global Inquiry'. Special issues, *JSAH*. Part I, 61, no. 3 (September 2002): 333–96; Part II, 61, no. 4 (December 2002): 509–58; Part III, 62, no. 1 (March 2003): 75–124.

Chastel, André, Jean Bony, Marcal Durliat, et al. *Pour un temps. Henri Focillon.* Paris: Centre Georges Pompidou, 1986.

Coffin, David R. *Pirro Ligorio: The Renaissance Artist, Architect and Antiquarian.* University Park, Pa.: Pennsylvania State University Press, 2004.

Cohen, Jean-Louis. 'Scholarship or Politics? Architectural History and the Risks of Autonomy'. *JSAH* 67, no. 3 (September 2008): 325–9.

Conway, Hazel, & Rowan Roenisch. *Understanding Architecture: An Introduction to Architecture and Architectural History.* London and New York: Routledge, 1994.

Cresti, Carlo. 'L'esercizio della Storia dell'architettura'. *Atti della Accademia delle arti del disegno 2007–2008* 14 (2008): 45–8.

Curuni, Alessandro. 'Gustavo Giovannoni. Pensieri e principi di restauro architettonica'. In *La cultura del restauro. Teorie e fondatori*, ed. Stella Casiello, 267–90. Venice: Marsilio, 1996.

Décultot, Élisabeth. *Johann Joachim Winckelmann. Enquête sur la genèse de l'histoire de l'art*. Paris: Presses universitaires de France, 2000.

Delbeke, Maarten, Evonne Levy & Steven F. Ostrow. 'Prolegomena to the Interdisciplinary Study of Bernini's Biographies'. In *Bernini's Biographies*, ed. Delbeke, Levy & Ostrow, 1–72. University Park, Pa.: Pennsylvania State University Press, 2007.

Donahue, Neil H. *Invisible Cathedrals: The Expressionist Art History of Wilhelm Worringer*. University Park, Pa.: Pennsylvania State University Press, 1995.

Draper, Peter (ed.). *Reassessing Nikolaus Pevsner*. Aldershot: Ashgate, 2003.

Dulio, Roberto. *Introduzione a Bruno Zevi*. Rome: Laterza, 2008.

Dunn, Richard M. *Geoffrey Scott and the Berenson Circle: Literary and Aesthetic Life in the Early 20th Century*. Lewiston, NY: Edwin Mellen Press, 1998.

Fairbank, Wilma. *Liang and Lin: Partners in Exploring China's Architectural Past*. Philadelphia: University of Pennsylvania Press, 1994.

Frankl, Paul. *Die Entwicklungsphasen der neuer Baukunst*. Stuttgart: B. G. Teubner, 1915. Engl. edn, *Principles of Architectural History: The Four Phases of Architectural Style*, trans. & ed. James F. O'Gorman. Cambridge, Mass.: MIT Press, 1968.

Georgiadis, Sokratis. *Sigfried Giedion. Eine intellektuelle Biographie*. Zurich: Eidgenössische Technische Hochschule, Institut für Geschichte und Theorie der Architektur, 1989. Engl. edn, *Sigfried Giedion: An Intellectual Biography*, trans. Colin Hall. Edinburgh: Edinburgh University Press, 1993.

Ghelardi, Maurizio, & Max Seidel (eds.). *Jacob Burckhardt. Storia della cultura, storia dell'arte*. Venice: Marsilio, 2002.

Ginzburg Carignani, Silvia (ed.). *Obituaries. 37 epitaffi di storici dell'arte nel Novecento*. Milan: Electa, 2008.

Halbertsma, Marlite. 'Nikolaus Pevsner and the End of a Tradition: The Legacy of Wilhelm Pinder'. *Apollo* (February 1993): 107–9.

Hancock, John E. *History in, of, and for Architecture*. Cincinnati, Ohio: The School of Architecture and Interior Design, University of Cincinnati, 1981.

Hart, Joan. 'Heinrich Wölfflin: An Intellectual Biography', Ph.D. diss., University of California, Berkeley, 1981.

Holly, Michael Ann. *Panofsky and the Foundations of Art History*. Ithaca, NY: Cornell University Press, 1984.

Hubert, Hans W. 'August Schmarsow, Hermann Grimm und die Gründung des Kunsthistorischen Instituts in Florenz'. In *Storia dell'arte e politica culturale intorno al 1900. La fondazione dell'Istituto Germanico di Storia dell'Arte di Firenze*, ed. Max Seidel, 339–58. Venice: Marsilio, 1999.

Iverson, Margaret. *Alois Riegl: Art History and Theory*. Cambridge, Mass.: MIT Press, 1993.

Jarzombek, Mark. *The Psychologizing of Modernity: Art, Architecture and History*. Cambridge: Cambridge University Press, 1999.

Kaufmann, Thomas DaCosta. *Toward a Geography of Art*. Chicago: University of Chicago Press, 2004.

King, Luise (ed.). *Architectur & Theorie: Produktion und Reflexion = Architecture & Theory: Production and Reflection*. Hamburg: Junius Verlag, 2009.

Kisacky, Jeanne. 'History and Science: Julien-David Leroy's Dualistic Method of Architectural History'. *JSAH* 60, no. 3 (September 2001): 260–89.

Kleinbauer, W. Eugene. *Modern Perspectives in Western Art History: An Anthology of 20th-Century Writings on the Visual Arts*. New York: Holt, Reinhart & Winston, 1971.

Kleinbauer, W. Eugene, & Thomas P. Slavens. *Research Guide to the History of Western Art*. Chicago: American Library Association, 1982.

Kohane, Peter. 'Interpreting Past and Present: An Approach to Architectural History'. *Architectural Theory Review* 2, no. 1 (1997): 30–7.

Kruft, Hanno-Walter. *Geschichte der Architekturtheorie von der Antike bis zur Gegenwart*. Munich: Beck, 1985. Engl. edn, *A History of Architectural Theory from Vitruvius to the Present*, trans. Ronald Taylor, Elsie Callander & Antony Wood. New York: Princeton Architectural Press, 1994.

Lagae, Johan, Marc Schoonderbeek, Tom Avermaete & Andrew Leach (eds.). 'Posities. Gedeelde gebieden in historiografie en ontwerp-praktijk = Positions: Shared Territories in Historiography and Practice'. Special issue, *Oase* 69 (2006).

Leach, Andrew. *Manfredo Tafuri: Choosing History*. Ghent: A&S Books, 2007.

Leach, Andrew, Antony Moulis & Nicole Sully (eds.). *Shifting Views: Essays on the Architectural History of Australia and New Zealand*. St Lucia, Qld: University of Queensland Press, 2008.

Legault, Régean. 'Architecture and Historical Representation'. *JAE* 44, no. 4 (August 1991): 200–5.

Lienert, Matthias. *Cornelius Gurlitt (1850 bis 1938): Sechs Jahrzehnte Zeit- und Familiengeschichte in Briefen.* Dresden: Thelem, 2008.

Lin Zhu. *Jianzhushi Liang Sicheng* [Architect Liang Sicheng]. Tianjin: Tianjin kexue jishu chubanshe, 1997.

—— *Koukai Lu Ban de damen: Zhongguo yingzao xueshe shilü* [Opening the Gate of Lu Ban: A Brief History of the Society for Research in Chinese Architecture]. Beijing: Zhongguo jainzhu gongye chubanshe, 1995.

Luca, Monica (ed.). *La critica operativa e l'architettura.* Milan: Edizioni Unicopli, 2002.

Macarthur, John. 'Some Thoughts on the Canon and Exemplification in Architecture.' *Form/Work: An Interdisciplinary Journal of Design and the Built Environment* 5 (2000): 33–45.

MacDougall, Elisabeth Blair (ed.). *The Architectural Historian in America: A Symposium in Celebration of the Fiftieth Anniversary of the Founding of the Society of Architectural Historians*, Studies in the History of Art 35, Center for Advanced Study in the Visual Arts Symposium Papers 19. Washington, DC: National Gallery of Art; Hanover, NH, and London: University Press of New England, 1990.

McKean, John. 'Sir Banister Fletcher: Pillar to Post-Colonial Readings'. *Journal of Architecture* 11, no. 2 (2006): 167–204.

Michel, André. 'L'enseignement de Louis Courajod'. *Leçons professées à l'École du Louvre (1887–1896)*, vol. III, *Origines de l'art moderne*, ed. Henry Lemonnier & André Michel, v–xvii. Paris: Alphonse Picard et Fils.

Midant, Jean-Paul. *Au Moyen Age avec Viollet-le-Duc.* Paris: Parangon, 2001.

Millon, Henry A. 'History of Architecture: How Useful?' *AIA Journal* 34, no. 6 (December 1960): 23–5.

Nalbantoğlu, Gülsüm. 'Towards Postcolonial Openings: Re-reading Sir Banister Fletcher's *History of Architecture*'. *Assemblage* 35 (1998): 6–17.

Otero-Pailos, Jorge. 'Photo[historio]graphy: Christian Norberg-Schulz's Demotion of Textual History'. *JSAH* 66, no. 2 (June 2007): 220–41.

Pächt, Otto. *Methodisches zur kunsthistorischen Praxis*, ed. Jorg Oberhaidacher, Arthur Rosenauer & Gertraut Schikola. Munich: Prestel, 1977. Engl. edn, *The Practice of Art History: Reflections on Method*, trans. David Britt. London: Harvey Miller, 1999.

Patetta, Luciano (ed.). *Storia dell'architettura. Antologia critica.* Milan: Etas, 1975.

Paul, Jürgen. *Cornelius Gurlitt: Ein Leben für Architektur, Kunstgeschichte, Denkmalpflege und Städtebau*. Dresden: Hellerau-Verlag, 2003.

Payne, Alina A. 'Rudolf Wittkower and Architectural Principles in the Age of Modernism'. *JSAH* 53, no. 3 (September 1994): 322–42.

Pevsner, Nikolaus. *Ruskin and Viollet-le-Duc: Englishness and Frenchness in the Appreciation of Gothic Architecture*. London: Thames & Hudson, 1969.

—— *Some Architectural Writers of the Nineteenth Century*. Oxford: Clarendon Press, 1972.

—— 'The Term "Architect" in the Middle Ages'. *Speculum* 17, no. 4 (October 1942): 549–62.

Pfisterer, Ulrich (ed.). *Klassiker der Kunstgeschichte*, 2 vols. Munich: Beck, 2008.

Podro, Michael. *The Critical Historians of Art*. New Haven, Conn.: Yale University Press, 1982.

Pollack, Martha (ed.). *The Education of the Architect: Historiography, Urbanism, and the Growth of Architectural Knowledge. Essays Presented to Stanford Anderson*. Cambridge, Mass.: MIT Press, 1997.

Pommier, Edouard. *Winkelmann, inventeur de l'histoire de l'art*. Paris: Gallimard, 2003.

Porphyrios, Demitri (ed.). 'On the Methodology of Architectural History'. Special issue, *Architectural Design* 51, nos. 6–7 (1981).

Pozzi, Mario & Enrico Mattioda. *Giorgio Vasari. Storico e critico*. Florence: Leo S. Olschki, 2006.

Preziosi, Donald (ed.). *The Art of Art History: A Critical Anthology*. Oxford History of Art. Oxford: Oxford University Press, 1998.

Ranaldi, Antonella. *Pirro Ligorio e l'interpretazione delle ville antiche*. Rome: Quasar, 2001.

Rosso, Michela. *La storia utile. Patrimonio e modernità di John Summerson e Nikolaus Pevsner, Londra, 1928–1955*. Turin: Edizioni di Comunità, 2001.

Salmon, Frank (ed.). *Summerson and Hitchcock: Centenary Essays on Architectural Historiography*. Studies in British Art 16. New Haven and London: Yale University Press, 2006.

Schlosser, Julius. *Die Kunstliteratur. Ein Handbuch zur Quellenkunde der neueren Kunstgeschichte*. Vienna: Anton Schroll, 1924.

—— 'The Vienna School of the History of Art: Review of a Century of Austrian Scholarship in German' (1934), trans. & ed.

Karl Johns. *Journal of Art Historiography* 1 (December 2009): 1–50. online at www.gla.ac.uk/departments/arthistoriography.

Scrivano, Paolo. *Storia di un'idea di architettura moderna: Henry-Russell Hitchcock e l'International Style.* Milan: FrancAngeli, 2001.

Seligman, Claus. 'Architectural History: Discipline or Routine?' *JAE* 34, no. 1 (Autumn 1980): 14–19.

Starace, Francesco, Pier Giulio Montano & Paolo Di Caterina. *Panofsky, von Simson, Woelfflin. Studi di teoria e critica dell'architettura.* Naples: Fratelli Napolitani, 1982.

Summers, David. 'Art History Reviewed II: Heinrich Wölfflin's "Kunstgeschichtliche Grundbegriffe", 1915'. *Burlington Magazine* 151, no. 1276 (July 2009): 476–9.

Tafuri, Manfredo. 'Architettura e storiografia. Una proposto di metodo'. *Arte Veneta* 29 (1975): 276–82.

—— *Teorie e storia dell'architettura.* Rome and Bari: Laterza, 1968. Engl. edn, *Theories and History of Archietecture*, trans. Giorgio Verrecchia from 4th Italian edn (1976) London: Granada, 1980.

Talenti, Simona. *L'histoire de l'architecture en France. Émergence d'une discipline (1863–1914).* Paris: Picard, 2000.

Testa, Fausto. *Winckelmann e l'invenzione della storia dell'arte. I modelli e la mimesi.* Bologna: Minerva, 1999.

Thomas, Helen. 'Invention in the Shadow of History: Joseph Rykwert at the University of Essex'. *JAE* 58, no. 2 (2004): 39–45.

Tournikiotis, Panayotis. *The Historiography of Modern Architecture.* Cambridge, Mass.: MIT Press, 1999.

Trachtenberg, Marvin. 'Some Observations on Recent Architectural History'. *Art Bulletin* 70, no. 2 (1988): 208–41.

Van Impe, Ellen. 'Architectural Historiography in Belgium, 1830–1914'. Ph.D. diss., Katholieke Universiteit Leuven, 2008.

—— 'Architectural History on Show: Retrospective Architectural History Exhibitions and Nineteenth Century Architectural History in Belgium'. *Fabrications* 16, no. 1 (June 2006): 63–89.

Vidler, Anthony. *Histories of the Immediate Present: Inventing Architectural Modernism.* Cambridge, Mass.: MIT Press, 2008.

Watkin, David. *The Rise of Architectural History.* London: Architectural Press, 1980.

Westfall, Carroll W. & Robert Jan van Pelt. *Architectural Principles in the Age of Historicism.* New Haven, Conn.: Yale University Press, 1991.

Whiffen, Marcus (ed.). *The History, Theory and Criticism of Architecture: Papers from the 1964 AIA-ACSA Teacher Seminar.* Cambridge, Mass.: MIT Press, 1965.

Whitely, Nigel. *Reyner Banham: Historian of the Immediate Future.* Cambridge, Mass.: MIT Press, 2002.

Wölfflin, Heinrich. *Kunstgeschichtliche Grundbegriffe. Das Problem der Stilentwicklung in der neueren Kunst.* Munich: Bruckmann, 1915. Engl. edn, *Principles of Art History: The Problem of Development of Style in Later Art,* trans. M. Hottinger from 7th German edn. New York: Dover, 1950.

Wood, Christopher (ed.). *The Vienna School Reader: Politics and Art Historical Method in the 1930s.* New York: Zone Books, 2000.

Wright, Gwendolyn & Janet Parks (eds.). *The History of Architecture in American Schools of Architecture, 1865–1975.* New York: Temple Hoyne Buell Center for the Study of American Architecture and Princeton Architectural Press, 1990.

Younés, Samir. *The True, the Fictive, and the Real: The Historical Dictionary of Architecture of Quatremère de Quincy.* London: Andreas Papadakis, 1999.

Index of names

CPSIA information can be obtained
at www.ICGtesting.com
Printed in the USA
FSOW02n0925271116
27861FS